75 Ways to Happiness

A Collection of Value-Based Stories

J.M. Mehta

V&S PUBLISHERS

Published by:

F-2/16, Ansari road, Daryaganj, New Delhi-110002
☎ 23240026, 23240027 • *Fax:* 011-23240028
Email: info@vspublishers.com • *Website:* www.vspublishers.com

Branch: Hyderabad
5-1-707/1, Brij Bhawan (Beside Central Bank of India Lane)
Bank Street, Koti, Hyderabad - 500 095
☎ 040-24737290
E-mail: vspublishershyd@gmail.com

Follow us on:

All books available at **www.vspublishers.com**

© **Copyright:** *V&S PUBLISHERS*
ISBN 978-93-815885-4-3
Edition: 2012

The Copyright of this book, as well as all matter contained herein (including illustrations) rests with the Publisher. No person shall copy the name of the book, its title design, matter and illustrations in any form and in any language, totally or partially or in any form. Anybody doing so shall face legal action and will be responsible for damages.

Printed at: Param Offseters, Okhla, New Delhi-110020

Publisher's Note

It's often said that Values, Morals and Ethics are intricately tied together. Values are what we learn from childhood; Morals are the intrinsic beliefs developed over our lifespan and Ethics are how we actually behave in the face of difficult situations that test our moral fibre. Hence, imbibing the right values in life is a must for everyone, who seeks happiness and bliss.

It is true that in our busy life schedule, we hardly get time to think and understand the significance of values, such as honesty, sincerity, faith, kindness, etc. Nonetheless, these values form the basis of our lives, families or the society, as a whole. We can inculcate these values by keeping a good company or by reading some good books teaching us the right values and morals of life for becoming a good person.

The book, *75 Ways to Happiness*, is a collection of such value-based stories in which each story teaches us some good value of life, as mentioned above through a short and interesting incident which we can easily relate to our day to day life. There is a box at the end of each story named "Something Extra" which highlights the moral or the value hidden in the story. The language used in the book is simple and lucid, and thus it can reach and enlighten people of almost all age groups.

Hope you enjoy reading these fascinating stories, and learn from them the values that can bring happiness into your lives...

Preface

A few years ago, I came across a book in English--titled 'Chicken Soup for the Souls....' It was one of the best sellers of that time. For me, its title appeared both interesting as well as funny! Different versions of this book have been published with similar titles. However, the 'chicken soup' remained the main ingredient. Each book contained different stories about efforts made by people in different spheres of life. Most of these stories were interesting and inspiring.

What intrigued me about this book was its funny title – 'Chicken soup for the Souls!' I wondered why the soul should be made to feed on the 'chicken soup'. I could not reconcile with the thought that the souls in Europe, America or elsewhere were fond of non-vegetarian food.

Anyway, without the best intention to enter into any controversy in this matter, I must admit that I was also inspired to collect relevant stories with an Indian or oriental background. Consequently, I have been able to compile a collection of 162 such micro-stories – thanks to the persistent efforts of several years. Out of these, about 75 stories have been compiled in this book. The main function of these stories is to ignite the process of thinking in relation to the various situations arising in human life. The reader may align himself with a story and deduce morals which may enable him to confront his own problems and find appropriate solutions.

I hope the stories contained in this book, some of which are true while others are fictitious, should serve as a healthy tonic to the minds and the souls of all general readers.

However, the stuff is pure vegetarian, but no less nutritious!

Alexander and the Saint

The Broken Myth of Owning the World!

After conquering many countries, Emperor Alexander invaded India, where he met a naked saint, whose words opened the Conqueror's eyes!

Alexander on seeing the naked saint told him, "You have nothing." The saint laughed and said: "The whole universe is mine. I have it

without invading it." Alexander said, "How can anyone win the world without conquering it?" The saint replied: "I have won over the Creator of this world. When I own the creator, the whole creation is mine. The way of my conquest is different from yours. I conquer, not by sword, but by surrendering myself!" Alexander was impressed by this reply and felt very pleased. Alexander said, "I too have conquered the world." In response the saint said, "Just imagine for a while that you are lost deep in a desert and are extremely thirsty. Then I appear before you with a jug of water and offer the same to you for a price. In case, you are about to die for water, how much of your kingdom can you give me for a jug of life saving water."

Alexander replied: "I shall be prepared to give half of my kingdom."

The saint said: "Suppose I do not sell my water at that price." Alexander told that he would be ready to give his whole kingdom to save his life. The saint laughed and said: "Then, in that case, only one jug of water is the price of your whole kingdom for which you have wasted your entire life."

These words of the saint had great impact on the mind of Alexander that he gave up the idea of further conquests. This incident which changed his thinking was also one of the reasons which prompted him to return to his country.

Something Extra

- Never insist that only you are right.
- Words of arrogance originate from poor wisdom.
- Practise Simple Living and High Thinking.

The Light of Devotion

Difference between pretence and serious work will show up any day!

In order to show off their love and respect to Lord Buddha, rich devotees used to light costly lamps as offerings to him. A very poor woman, who had great love and respect for Buddha, noticed this and she too wanted to offer a lamp, but was too poor to buy one.

Nevertheless, she worked hard, begged and raised a small amount to buy an earthen lamp and filled it with some oil and small cotton wick. She prayed earnestly and begged Buddha to accept her humble offering. Next morning, it came to the notice of one of the chief disciples of lord Buddha that barring a little earthen lamp, all other lamps were extinguished. The little earthen lamp was still burning and was full of oil and wick. He communicated this strange happening to the Lord, who said, "This lamp is lit with the wick of devotion and the oil of sincerity. Nothing will put out this light. Let us all bestow our inner selves with this type of light."

Here, the light is the symbol of inner peace, love and devotion. And all human beings should fill their inner self with light like this.

Something Extra

- Resource-crunch should never be a constraint in starting an endeavour.
- Selfless devotion ultimately leads to big rewards.
- Attitude for hard work rather than show off pays off at the end.

Unselfish Love

The Milk of Human kindness knows no barriers and animals are no exception!

This is a touching story of a very kind person who bought two pups for a distant relative who lived in far off city. He carried the pups by train to deliver them to his relative.

On his way to the relative's house, after getting down from the train in a hired taxi, he asked the driver to halt at a roadside *dhaba* (eatery) to

feed the pups with some milk. The taxi stopped in front of a hut which was a small *dhaba*. The gentleman asked the owner for some milk for the pups. An old woman came out and picked up the pups with great love and fed them fondly with milk in a bowl. She told the man that she too had two pups but they were killed by a careless driver on the roadside. The old woman showered all the love and affection on the two pups even though they did not belong to her. Admiring her kind attitude, the man was greatly surprised at the conduct of the poorly dressed old woman and offered her money for the milk. She did not accept the money, washed the pups, kissed them and gave them to the owner reluctantly. She said, "Sir, they also have life, never be cruel to them." There were tears in her eyes when she said these words and looked at the pups with great love as the man took them away. The love and affection that old woman showered on the pups, was like the love from a mother's heart for her own children, untainted and unselfish!

Something Extra

- Always be kind to your fellow beings including pet animals.
- Mother-like love is supreme and has a healing touch.
- Cultivate the habit of doing small favours without any monetary interest.

A Memorable Gift

Patience is a shield against future regrets!

A young man was very fond of a sports car, exhibited in a dealer's showroom, and told his rich father about it. What followed can be interesting....

At his graduation, the young man expected his father to gift that car to him. On the morning of his graduation, his father called him and gave

his son a gift box. When the son opened it, he found a holy book inside. Angrily he shouted, "With all your riches, you give me just a book!" and left the house and the book.

After several years, the young man became a rich businessman. He realised that he must get back to his father, who had grown old. Just then, he received a telegram informing him of his father's death. When he returned to his father's house, he came to know that his father had willed him all his property and possessions. As he was searching through important papers, he found the same holy book which his father had gifted him at his graduation. Beneath the book he found an envelope, taped and contained papers for a sports car, with the dealer's name. On the papers, the date of graduation was written, along with words, 'PAID IN FULL' what a surprise!

Something Extra

- Respect Elders' Opinions and Wisdom.
- Never jump to sudden conclusions.
- Think, analyse and react patiently.
- Never create situations that may cause regret in future.

Who is Your Real Friend?

Noble Deeds double up as Friends and Fame in life!

A person was accidentally framed for a crime that he did not commit. He was issued a warrant.

He had three friends and he asked one of them to testify to his innocence as a witness. The friend said. "I cannot move out of this house.

But can help you only from here." He, therefore, had to approach others. The second friend said, "I can come up to the doorway of the court but will not enter the witness box."

The third friend said. "I will speak for you, wherever you want me to come." This is the story of our life. The first is PROPERTY which can bear witness only within the house. The second is RELATIVES who would come till the cemetery. The third friend is one's own virtues and noble deeds which continue to shine even after death and stand witness for a long time to come.

The good thoughts and actions of life
will serve as good friends who will
bring peace and progress.

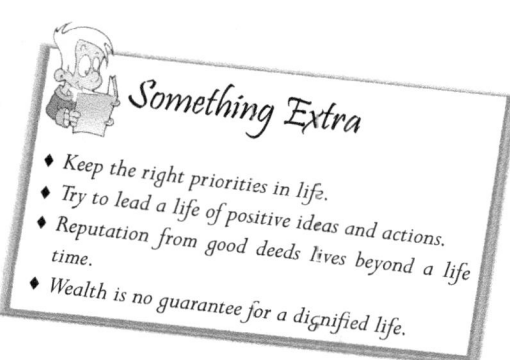

Something Extra

- Keep the right priorities in life.
- Try to lead a life of positive ideas and actions.
- Reputation from good deeds lives beyond a life time.
- Wealth is no guarantee for a dignified life.

The Right Medicine

Solutions stand disguised in the problem itself!

A very fat lady, having problems in walking, decided to consult a doctor to get medication to reduce her fat. The doctor asked her a few questions and told her to come after two days so that he could consult his books and give her the right medicine.

The lady came after two days and the doctor told her, "Madam, I have consulted my books and have come to the conclusion that you will die in the next ten days. Therefore, there is no use giving you any medicine!" The woman got scared and went home. She was very sad and stopped eating and drinking. Due to this, in ten days, she lost a lot of weight and became thin. But she did not die so she went to the doctor after ten days to tell him that she was still alive. The doctor asked her, "Are you fat or thin" She replied, "I am thin and lost all my fat because of the fear of dying." The doctor said, "That was the right medicine for you."

The lady went home happy and satisfied.

Something Extra

- Never wait for a solution till a problem completely overwhelms you.
- Preventing a disease is easier than curing it.
- Anxiety delays action and is no solution to a problem.

Rich Man vs. Poor Man

Excuse is the alibi of lazy and selfish!

A poor man was struggling to find money to marry off his daughter. So he approached a rich man for some money. Did the rich man help him?

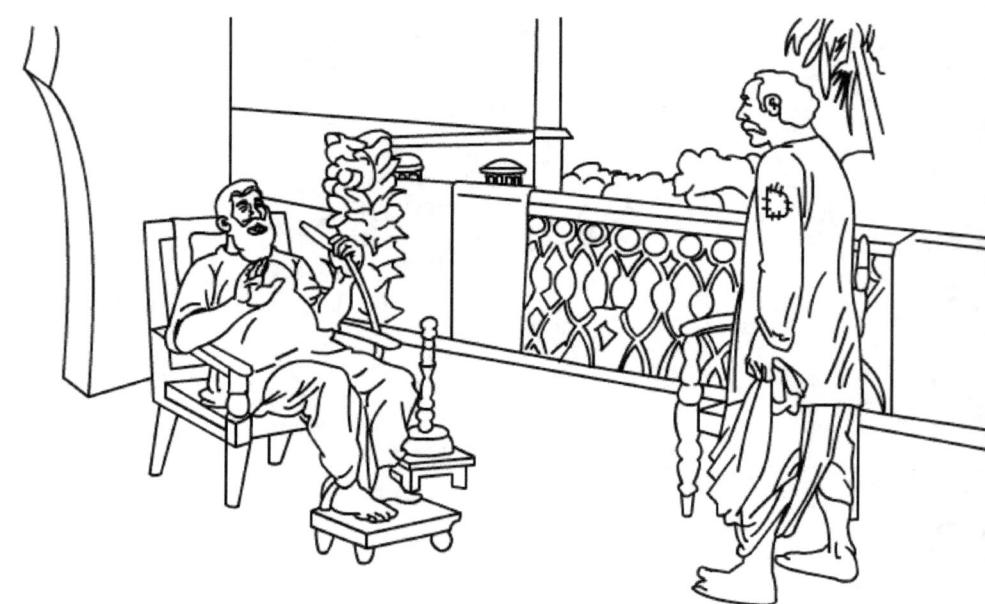

The rich man was reluctant to part with his money so he put him off saying, "I don't have any spare money, now, please come after some days."

So the poor man went away and returned after a few days and repeated his request.

The rich man said, "I have money now, but I do not have my cashier to give it to you. So please come after some days."

The poor man got the hint and went away saying, "I thought a rich man is also a man!"

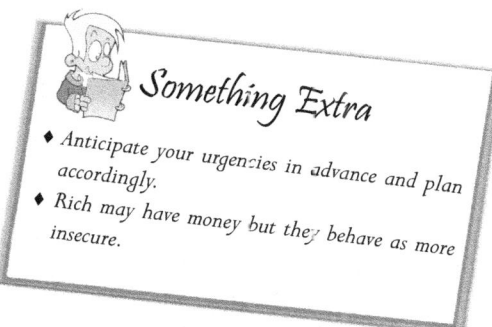

Something Extra
- Anticipate your urgencies in advance and plan accordingly.
- Rich may have money but they behave as more insecure.

A True Devotee

Ignore the acts of the wicked and jealous and never react in their language!

Eknath was a true devotee of God. He would go to the temple every day, after taking bath. One day, when he was on the way to the temple, a jealous man spat on his face. Did Eknath reply violently to this act of aggression?

Eknath went back home, took bath and again that person spat on him. In this way, the man continued to soil Eknath one hundred times; Eknath in turn took bath a hundred times and did not say anything to the wicked man. Finally, the wicked person who was ashamed and remorseful sought Eknath's forgiveness. Eknath simply remarked, "God wanted me to take bath a hundred times." He showed no ill will against the man so much so that he finally became the disciple of the holy man. This is how you can win over those who are on the wrong path.

Something Extra

- Virtue always triumphs over the wicked.
- Allow the wicked to understand the evil and give them an opportunity to change.
- Real wisdom lies in not getting provoked by the pranks of idiots.

The Sinner and the Christ

Assess one's own worth before judging others!

A woman, a bad character and a sinner was brought before Jesus Christ with her hands tied to the back with a furious mob shouting at her. Christ saved her from the angry crowd and showed her a divine path…

The woman was mobbed by the people who wanted to pronounce death punishment on her. Jesus first looked at her and told the crowd, "If

she is not denying acts of sinning then she surely deserves punishment." At this, the crowd shouted. "Death to her, punish her."

Jesus said. "Yes, she should be punished as per your wish, and so get ready to hit her with five stones each." Everybody picked up stones to hit her. The woman was terrified.

Then Jesus said loudly, "Beware! Only that man will hit her first, who is not a sinner himself! In case any sinner hits her, he will be punished."

Hearing this, the crowd lowered their hands. Tears rolled down the woman's eyes and she looked towards Jesus. The crowd, which was shouting for punishment started retreating with their heads down. Jesus untied the knot and released her. Jesus said: "You are free to go wherever you want. God is all merciful. You can seek his forgiveness for your sins in all sincerity."

The woman was ashamed and cried out in full force as if her sins were being drowned in the flow of tears as regret and repentance! Such was the magic of a saint's compassion!

Something Extra

- Think before passing judgement on others.
- Work positively to raise ones' own worth.
- Forgive the erred and give opportunity to improve.

A Man of Courage

Determination dwarfs all handicaps in life!

A lady commuter was standing at the roadside looking for a cycle-rickshaw. Suddenly, a rickshaw-puller, clad in *kurta pyjama*, appeared and said, "Madam, are you looking for a rickshaw?" The ride in that rickshaw revealed the noble side of that poor man!

She took the rickshaw and found that the man plying it was very alert and careful while plying it unlike many others. She posed a few questions to the man but he was not talking much. There must be a reason to it....

Then the lady noticed that he had no left leg and he was frequently pulling up the *pyjama* from the left side. The lady felt sympathetic and probed more about him. This time he told his story. He was originally a farmer from Bihar, who lost his left leg in an accident. Deciding not to become a burden on his family, he moved to Delhi along with his wife. He hired a rickshaw on a monthly basis and started earning. His wife too started earning as a housemaid. By this time, his wife was pregnant and both wanted to give their child a good education and groom the kid as a responsible citizen. The man shared many such matters with her and that impressed the lady. When her destination was drawing close, seeing the road in bad shape, she offered to get down a little ahead of her house. But this man insisted on dropping her at the gate of her house. The lady admired his good behaviour and courage and paid him well. He thanked the lady and went away happy and smiling.

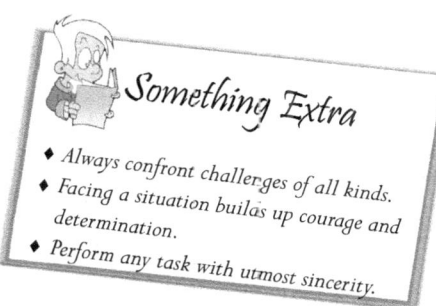

Something Extra

- Always confront challenges of all kinds.
- Facing a situation builds up courage and determination.
- Perform any task with utmost sincerity.

Let us not Imitate Others

The principal mark of a genius is not perfection, but originality!

This is what late Douglas Malloch said:
If you can't be a pine on the top of the hill be a scrub in the valley – but be the best little scrub by the side of the rill;

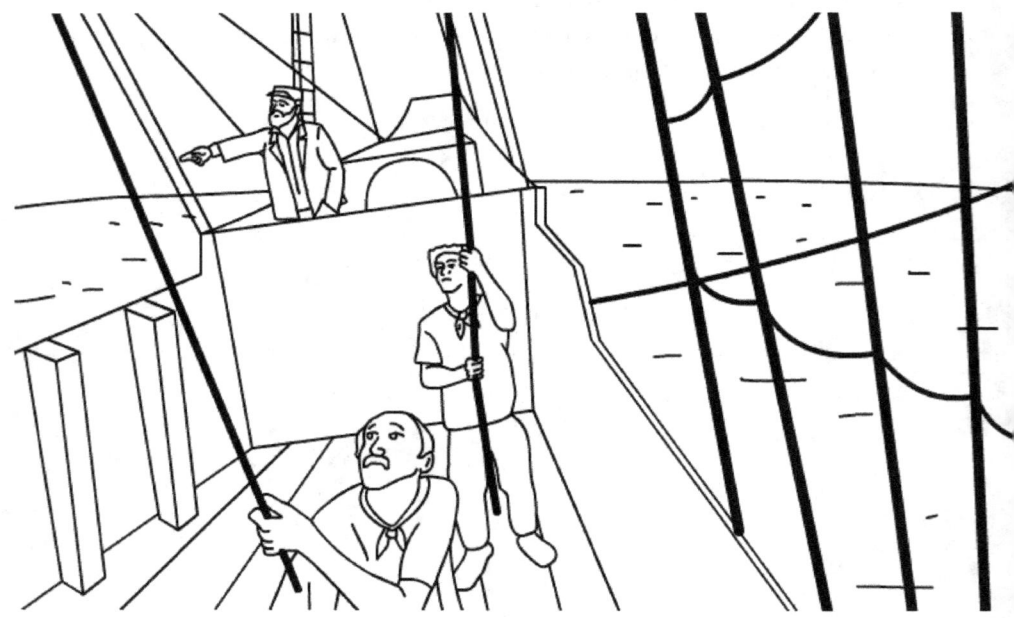

Be a bush if you can't be a tree.
If you can't be a bush be a bit of the grass,
and some highway some happier make;
if you can't be a muskie then just be a bass-
but the liveliest bass in the lake!

We can't all be captains, we've got to be crew,
there's something for all of us here.
There's big work to do and there's lesser to do,
and the task we must do is the near."

If you can't be a highway then just be a trail,
if you can't be the sun be a star;
it isn't by size that you win or you fail-
Be the best of whatever you are!

Let us not imitate others.
Let us find ourselves and be ourselves.

Something Extra
- Originality is the key to success..
- Always strive for perfection.
- One cannot excel if one imitates.

Love of God

Risk of Acting as God's Advocate!

This is a story about Prophet Moses, who heard a voice from a shepherd, saying: "Oh God, where are you? How can I stitch your clothes; mend your shoes and offer you milk?" Moses' annoyance at the shepherd's pleadings with the God led to an interesting revelation!

The shepherd's voice was overflowing with love. Moses was greatly surprised to hear all these and took it as blasphemy. He came to the shepherd and said, "How dare you speak like this? Do you think God is human who can drink your milk and get the hair combed by you! Your talk amounts to insulting our religion."

The shepherd became speechless and wondered whether he had said anything wrong! Heartbroken, he wept and apologised to the prophet and went away. Moses felt happy the he had taught a lesson to the fool. Suddenly a voice thundered, "Moses, why did you interfere between me and my child; who authorised you to separate the lover from the beloved. Why did you drive my faithful devotee away from me? I have no need for praises and worship. It is the sincerity of heart that alone interests me." Moses felt humbled and went after the shepherd. He found him meditating by a spring, calm and compassionate. He was truly full of love of God.

Something Extra
- Double check before speaking on behalf of any authority.
- Never misinterpret messages to suit personal interests.
- Always encourage creative people.

A Story of Ideal Love

Accepting people as they are develops trust and understanding!

A married couple loved each other intensely. A few months after marriage, the wife read an article on the ways to strengthen marital relations. She wanted to apply that knowledge in her own life. What followed was interesting....

On the basis of that knowledge, she suggested her husband to make a list of all negative points so that they can discuss candidly and sort out differences. The husband had no objection. Next day, the wife brought out her long list and started reading. While reading, she noticed that her husband's eyes were filled with tears!

She asked, "Anything wrong?" He replied, "No, please carry on." The wife read out the list and kept it on the table, saying. "Now, you read out your list and we shall discuss." The husband said, "I don't have any list. I think you are o.k., the way you are. I don't want you to change for my sake." The wife was surprised and impressed by the straightforward answer which reflected his honest and deep love for her and his total acceptance of her. She wept and embraced him.

The husband-wife relationship lasts long on mutual love and understanding.

Something Extra
- Nobody is perfect.
- See the positive things first in a person.
- Approach people positively.

The Lighter Side

Smiles of Happiness and Smiles of Pretence Differ!

Three dead men were brought to the city morgue. All of them died with a smile on their face. The city police wanted to know the reason of the smile. The disclosed reasons may make you smile...

They discovered that each had a separate reason as in the following:-

The first body was that of a miser who died, counting money. He enjoyed his work very much, hence the smile! The second man was a gambler. While gambling, he had a winning hand of a large amount, and died of heart attack.

The third man was struck by lightning. But the sheen on his face was puzzling. It was later found out that he was a POLITICIAN! When he saw the flash of lightning, he thought he was being photographed; so he had to smile!

Something Extra

- Be genuine in your work.
- Never try to please for the sake of it.
- Make the mind joyful with a right occupation.

Sympathy - In a Cup of Tea

Genuine Care Speaks!

An old, emaciated man who underwent a bone marrow transplant was lying on a bed, sad and hopeless. His nurse came and said, "Hello, Mr. John, I am your nurse, Lily. Will you like to have some soup?" He refused; but the nurse had other ideas....

The man shook his head and said, "I want to sleep." Later, she came back with medicine which he took and sank back to his pillow. He did not react and the nurse went back with a feeling dejected.

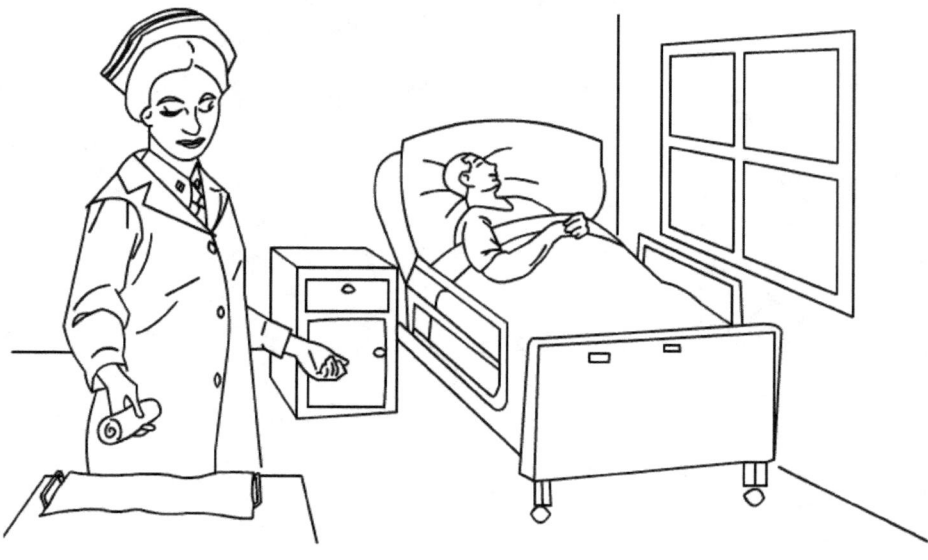

But the nurse did not lose heart. She went to the kitchen, and made two cups of tea, put on a tray and went to his room. She said politely, "Shall l have my tea in your room and also watch the T.V.?" He said, "yes, of course," but closed his eyes.

The nurse put on the T.V. and he opened his eyes and began watching the TV. She noticed this and said, "I have an extra cup of tea, if you care to have it." The man reacted favourably and said, "Just half a cup." Then both watched the T.V. in silence. When she was preparing to leave, he asked, "Will you come tomorrow?" she smiled and said, "Yes, I will and have tea with you again." He said, "I like that."

Next day, he had a full cup of tea and toast and looked better. The nurse talked to him and he felt encouraged. The third night he had two cups of tea and told the nurse about his job and the family. On the fourth night, he got out of the bed and sat in a chair. His routine continued as the nurse conversed with him politely and sympathetically. A few days later, he recovered and went back home.

Some months later, when the nurse went for shopping in a store, she heard a booming noise "Lily, it is nice to see you here." He was his old patient in the hospital. He introduced her to his wife and said, "She saved my life with her sweet talk and many cups of tea." He hugged her, thanked her, before parting company. This is how a nurse helped her patient to recover, with sweet conversation, compassion and many cups of tea!

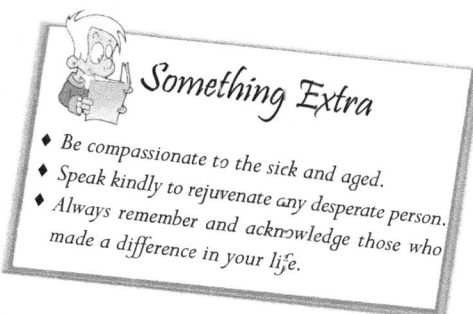

Something Extra

- Be compassionate to the sick and aged.
- Speak kindly to rejuvenate any desperate person.
- Always remember and acknowledge those who made a difference in your life.

The Hidden Power

Never Ignore Premonitions and Intuitions!

I, my wife, and our handicapped child used to go to a neighbouring park on Sundays, where my son would play and enjoy the green grassy environment. We all used to go in a small car and stay at the park for a few hours and then come back home happy. But one day, I had a strange experience....

Once I parked the car outside the forest garden and we all walked inside and sat on a grassy corner. Our small boy played for a while and fell asleep. We strolled in the park and when he woke up, had some refreshments and came to the parking lot. To my surprise, when I searched for the car-key in my pocket, it was missing! It was lost somewhere in and around the park, but where could I look for it in such a big park? Anyway, something goaded me to retrace my steps and go back to the place where we sat; still the key was not traceable. As I was about to turn around, I looked again towards the corner, where we sat. And to my surprise, I saw something shining and that was the key chain and the key. How did I get it when I was about to go away, disappointed!. Some hidden power indeed!

Something Extra

- *Be alert about your personal belongings.*
- *When something is lost, do not panic.*
- *Search widely without ruling out options.*

Beauty Beneath Ugliness

Poverty Hits only the Body Not the Mind!

An old woman was sitting on a bench in a public park. She looked very miserable – torn clothes; dirty hair and shabby looks. She had a paper-bag with her that carried her belongings. But she was happy with her past and a small boy discovered her kind heart……

Small squirrels would come near her feet and she would throw small pieces of bread which they would catch and run away. At this, she would burst into petty laughter. A woman and her small boy came that way but did not like to sit with her. But the old woman beckoned the boy who was watching her act of feeding the squirrels. He ran to her and both started feeding the small animals and together enjoyed many hearty laughs. Soon the mother also joined them and shared their joy and mirth.

Initially, both mother and her little boy did not like to share the bench with the ugly woman. Now they both sat with her and shared the fun. They discovered her human side as a generous and loving person. It was the beauty beneath the ugliness that attracted them. Appearances can become deceptive, sometimes!

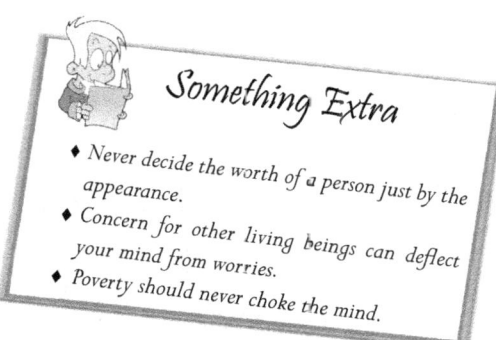

Something Extra

- Never decide the worth of a person just by the appearance.
- Concern for other living beings can deflect your mind from worries.
- Poverty should never choke the mind.

The Evil of Poverty

Love for the child and pangs of poverty!

This is the true story of a poor woman who had no option but to sell her baby for a few bucks. It is a message that there are many unfortunate mothers who struggle to feed their precious child!

A poor woman – an orphan, earned her living doing odd jobs. She

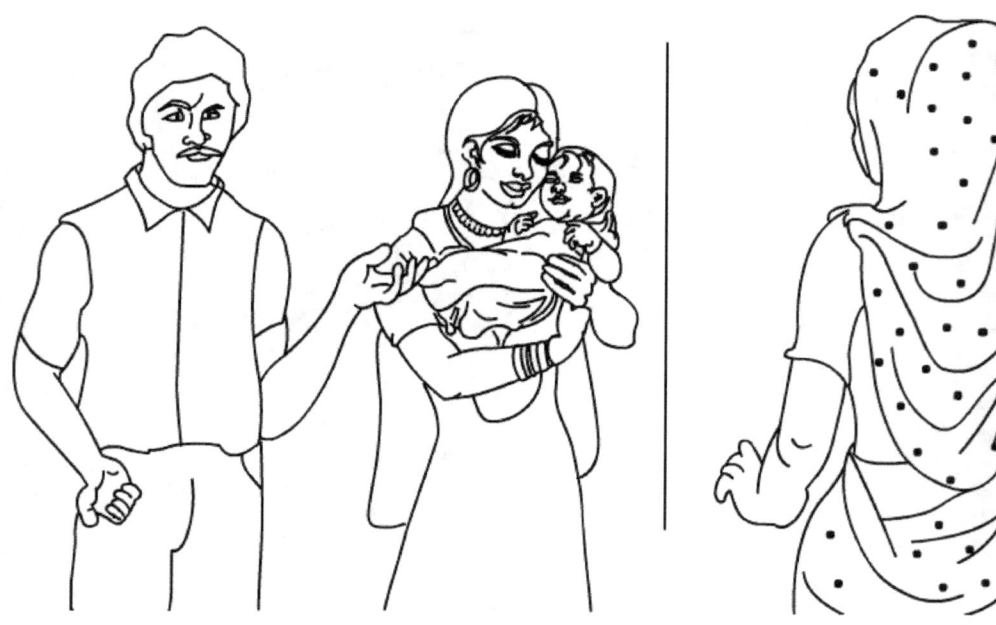

gave birth to a baby, and was living on the pavement. Driven by poverty and desperation, she did not want to keep the child and looked for someone who could take care of the baby.

She met a childless couple, who were willing to adopt the baby. The deal was struck for Rs. 2000/-. The news of the sale got public soon. People started questioning both the mother and the couple, who denied the sale and said that they had only given the money for food, etc. They had taken the child as a gesture of help and sympathy as otherwise it will not survive! However, the mother confessed having sold the baby since she could not keep it. Later she revealed that someone had promised to marry her, but backed out. She had, therefore, no option but to sell the child.

Something Extra

- Never give false promises to any one.
- A newborn always deserves a better life.
- Always be accountable for your actions.

The Hidden Hand of God

Instincts can be pointers to great things in the Future!

This is the story of a farmer's son, whose father led a righteous life. Right from his very childhood, the young boy had been displaying noble qualities despite formal education. In later life, his instincts made him a wise man.......

The farmer's son used to help his father in farming activities. One day, while working in the field, the son saw a large crab, which he picked up and brought home. He kept it in an earthen pot by the side of his bed and slept. By chance, a cobra entered the room and put its head into the pot. The crab caught the head of the snake and bit it hard and crushed it; as a result the cobra died.

On waking up, the young man was surprised to see the sequence of events. Many questions arose in his mind. "Why did I catch the crab and bring it home?" "How did the cobra come inside?, Why did the snake put its head into the pot, etc. It could have indeed bitten me? and so on." In his later life, this thoughtful boy became a YOGI and found answers to all his questions.

Something Extra
- There is a definite purpose behind all actions.
- Positive acts lead to positive results.
- Take time to assist elders in domestic work.

Justice of Grandson

Sometimes even children teach their ignorant parents!

An old, sick man used to live with his son and family. They used to have their meals together on the same table. But certain changes happened in the household....

In due course, the hands of the old man became weak and shaky and eating became difficult. Sometimes, the food would fall on the table or floor or clothes. His son and the daughter-in-law would get annoyed and

wanted to do something about it. They put a separate small table in the corner of the dining room, for feeding the old man. They also brought a wooden platter for serving the food since he had already broken some plates. The old man would eat his food, sitting in a corner all alone feeling humiliated. Tears would flow down his eyes.

The old man's five-year-old grandson was silently watching the plight of his grandfather. One day the boy was trying to make something out of some wooden scrap when his father asked, "Son, what are you doing?" The boy replied innocently, "I am trying to make a wooden platter for you and Mom, to eat food, when you grow old, like grandfather." The parents were shocked to hear this. They got the message and were full of remorse. Their eyes became moist with tears.

The same evening, they led their father gently to the same dining table, gave him good food and sought his forgiveness. The old man became happy and ate his food with the family as long as he lived. His son and daughter-in-law never showed any irritation if something fell from his shaky hands.

This is how a small child – a grandson got justice for his old grandfather who was being ill-treated by his son and daughter-in-law.

Something Extra

- Respect your parents and treat them with love and care.
- Present oneself as a good model to the child.
- Every action has an equal and opposite reaction.

A Brother's Concern

Small acts of kindness can save many lives!

   A small boy used to sit near a temple and sell flowers and garlands to the devotees. He used to sit from early morning till late night and try his best to sell flowers. There was a touching story behind his urge to sell flowers....

The boy would always approach a lady, who would visit the temple every day and beg her earnestly to buy flowers, but somehow she never did that. The boy would follow her again even when she came out of the temple. Other boys also sold flowers, but this boy was very persistent in selling his wares.

The same lady did not visit the temple for many days. However, she went there after a gap of many months and saw the same boy sitting there. But this time, he did not ask her to buy the flowers. He looked at the lady and did not utter a word. The lady found this strange and went over to him and asked, "Why did not you ask me to buy your flowers?" He replied, "Madam, why should I ask?. You are rich but can't spend ten rupees to buy a garland from me. But now I am not that desperate to sell. My sister was suffering from cancer. I used to sell garlands to buy medicines for her. She passed away a month ago!"

The lady was so overwhelmed that she bought all his flowers. However, she repented that she did not buy any, when the boy was trying very hard to sell it. Time lost never comes back.

Never hesitate to do a good deed.

Something Extra

- No individual should live like an island.
- Small helps can make the society more beautiful.
- Keep an eye on the outer world and be kind and generous.

When Lord Krishna Missed the Ghee

When humour drills in more common sense!

This is the story of a maid, Radha and the deity, Lord Krishna. Radha was working as a maid to one lady. After a few years, she got married and had a baby boy. The lady would visit her home regularly to provide some food for the mother and child.

One day, after taking bath, the lady's husband searched for *desighee* to light the lamp for the daily worship (puja) of Lord Krishna. He could not get it and asked his wife about it. She had given the whole packet of *ghee* to Radha, the maidservant for her nourishment. The husband was annoyed. To this she remarked jokingly, "My Radha needs the *ghee* more than your Krishna."

At this, both the husband and wife burst into laughter. Love for fellowmen is equivalent to the love of God. If we do service to the needy, it amounts to service of the Lord.

Something Extra

- Happiness doubles when you make someone happy.
- Never be a slave of personal comforts.
- Develop a sense of humour.

Be Polite, But Firm

Kind words taste like honey!

Harsh and impolite words can lead to hurt feelings and even hard fights. So it is good to be polite while speaking.

Once Bibi Ayesha, the youngest wife of Prophet Muhammad was shouting at someone as he could not complete some work. Prophet Muhammad heard this out and advised his young wife: "Ayesha, Allah has not provided us with a bone in the tongue. This is simply because

we need to talk to people softly and pleasingly." As spoken words have the potential to promote both love and hatred, it is always advisable to be polite.

We should follow the example of the Father of the Nation, Mahatma Gandhi, who would create magic by his use of simple and polite words. But there was firmness beneath his politeness and Gandhiji would convey the right message to the listener. So learn to be polite, but firm and keep a check on your anger. Such an attitude will save you from many unwanted problems.

Something Extra

- Harsh words give hard feelings.
- Speak soothingly and make it a habit.
- Polite words can still send a strong message.

A Lesson from a Beggar

For the really hungry, any food is sumptuous!

A spoilt teenager of some rich parents was very fussy about the taste of food provided to him. Even a slight variation in the quantity of salt in his food would enrage him and he would throw away the food!

His mother tried her best to prepare food according to his taste and liking, but he would always find fault and blame the mother. Both the parents would try to pacify him, but he would mostly get angry

and refuse to eat. This made the parents very unhappy, while he himself remained dissatisfied.

One day, he and his parents had to go to the railway station to see off his newly married sister. As they were waiting at the station for the departure of the train, his eyes fell on a poor beggar, who was in rags and sitting behind a pillow with his torn bag. He saw the beggar taking out a cup from the bag. He filled his cup with water from the water tap at the station and came back to the same place. Then he took out a dried *chapatti* from his bag,. He would dip the *chapatti* in the cup of water, so that it can get soft and then eat it. In this way, the hungry beggar ate up the whole of the *chapatti*.

The boy watched the beggar, very carefully, while he was eating his *chapatti*. This incident stayed in his mind and he started thinking deeply. The picture of the beggar eating his dried *chapatti* calmly by dipping in tasteless water kept flashing in his mind. On the other hand, he had the luxury of rich tasty food of all sorts and still was angry and dissatisfied. That night, he quietly ate whatever was prepared for dinner, without getting angry and making any complaint. The boy gct a lesson from the poor beggar. From that day, he became a changed person and never annoyed his parents with his rude behaviour.

Something Extra

- Earn your food from your hard work.
- Eat only when your are really hungry.
- You get the food you deserve.

A Matter of Faith

Mind Matters more than Holy Robes!

Once, a hermit (sanyasi) and a prostitute used to live in houses adjacent to each other. It so happened that both died on the same day. Lord YAMA's servants, who were sent to fetch them, were confused as to why they were asked to take the *sanyasi* to hell and the prostitute to heaven! But the mystery was removed later....

The order to shift the *sanyasi* to hell came despite his enjoying a good

reputation and the prostitute in ill fame because of her bad profession. Lord Yama's servants, or *Yamdoots* thought that there was some goof up! So they went to Chitragupta who was keeping all records for verification and guidance. Chitragupta verified and found that Lord YAMA'S orders were in order.

The fact was – their external appearances deceived the reality. Every morning when the *Sanyasi* used to chant the holy *mantras*, the prostitute living in the opposite house wanted to be present at the prayers, but could not do so because of her profession. So she would purify herself by crying out to remove her guilt. Since she yearned to participate in God's worship, she would put her ears against the walls of the *sanyasi's* house and fill herself with the holy thoughts of God sincerely praying that in her next life, she be given on opportunity to serve at a temple.

But the *sanyasi* had different thoughts. At night, when he would hear the sounds of dance and music in the opposite house, he would pity himself that he could not enjoy the pleasure there. So he cursed his lot as a *sanyasi* and longed to visit the house of the prostitute but could not do so because of his holy external garb!

So Chitragupta explained to the *Yamdoots* that in reality the *sanyasi* was living in a brothel and the prostitute lived in the temple because of their inner thoughts! So, it is the reality inside which matters and not the external appearances!

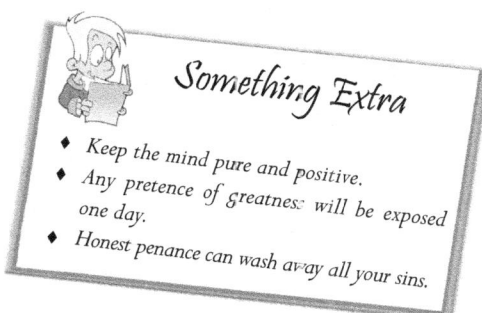

Something Extra

- Keep the mind pure and positive.
- Any pretence of greatness will be exposed one day.
- Honest penance can wash away all your sins.

Gender Discrimination

Loving children on the basis of gender is a crime!

Men and women are equal. But as the topmost creation of God, both are complementary to each other. However, our society rejoices at the birth of a male child and considers it superior to a female. Why so? The following story will be an eye-opener!

The only grown up son of a rich man went abroad to settle there in search of greener pastures, without informing his father and only sister.

He sold his movable property and flew overseas, with his wife. His aged and sick father was left to the care of his married daughter, who had to shift to her father's house to look after him. About a year later, the father became seriously ill and was admitted to a private hospital, where he died soon. The son was informed, he rushed back, paid the bills and performed all the death rites and returned overseas.

Most people criticised the son for abandoning his father at his old age. It was the daughter who came to help her old father even at the cost of disrupting her settled life in another city! Despite several such incidents, the society rules a son more precious than a daughter as the son is supposed to carry forward the family name. What a travesty of our family structure, which we are boasting to the outer world! The fact is, it is high time we avoided gender discrimination to create a just and better society.

Something Extra

- Treat all the children with the same amount of love.
- Provide them with equal opportunities.
- Never try to be a burden on any one.

Teamwork

Teamwork cuts the tedium of work!

A man lost his way while driving through the countryside. In his effort to find the right way, he accidentally drove off the road and fell into a pit. His car was stuck deep in the mud, though he was not injured. He went over to a nearby farm and sought help. He had an interesting experience.

A farmer there agreed to come to his rescue. He said, "Yes, my old mule, WARWICK can help." So the two men with a mule came to the pit. The farmer hitched the mule to the car and shouted, "Pull Pull, JACK, Pull Brown, Pull WARWICK," and in a second, the car was pulled out.

The man thanked the farmer, patted the mule and enquired, "Tell me, why did you call the other two names, while only Warwick was there?" The farmer smiled and replied, "The old Warwick is blind. When I call the other two names, he thinks that he is working as a part of a team, so he does not have to pull alone."

Thus the spirit of teamwork leads to success. Sometimes, belief is all that you need to do a job and success is assured.

Something Extra
- Solo work never gives good results.
- Work within a team.
- Nothing beats a team effort.

An Orphan and His Home

There is always a payback time!

Once, a three-month old abandoned baby was picked up by a team of young doctors, who ran an orphanage for poor children. From there, the child grew up and studied up to the high school. Unfortunately, the facilities at the home were turning worse due to the shortage of funds. How this misery affected that boy and how he addressed them is the crux of the story......

The young boy had a hard life in the orphanage. With the help of his other companions, he lodged a protest and fought for better facilities in the orphanage. Moved by their plight, the authorities provided funds and the conditions improved. The boy could not continue his studies as he had no means and therefore, sought employment in a bakery. Meanwhile, he also registered himself in the employment exchange. Sometime later, he was offered the job of a peon in the same orphanage, where he had spent his early childhood. He thought, it was an opportunity for him to improve the lot of children there. He worked hard and conditions improved. He loved and helped the children in all possible manner. Soon more children flocked to the same orphanage in view of the improved conditions. The abandoned child who was once brought as an orphan to the orphanage became the father figure to about 300 inmates. He volunteered to serve in the orphanage and made it his home as long as he lived.

Something Extra

- Turn protests into positive actions.
- Try to provide others with the facilities you missed.
- Work for improving the lot of others.

The Satvik Food

Eating the right food in the right manner!

According to the yogic texts, pure vegetarian food promotes love, purity and goodness, besides health and strength. That is why the practitioners of yogic culture and spiritual discipline are particular about what one should eat.

Such foods are called *satvik foods* which include fresh fruits, organic vegetables, whole wheat and pulses. Nuts, Intoxicants, cola, coffee, eggs, meat and strong spices are not included in this category.

Merely eating *satvik food* is not enough; the method of cooking should also be *satvik*. Deep frying should he avoided in any case. Cooking over low heat and steaming are better alternatives. *Satvik* principles also involve how to eat and how much to eat. Food should be chewed well and overeating should be avoided. *Satvik food* makes the mind clear and peaceful, and enables wisdom to flow freely and shine through the whole body. So *Satvik food* is the preferred food to nourish the mind and the soul.

Something Extra

- Maintain good food habits.
- Be quality conscious in your eating habits.
- Eat those food items that keep you healthy and energetic.

The Importance of Shoulders in Human Body

Supportive attitude develops leadership skills!

Once a mother asked her son, "What is the most important part of a human body?" The son thought of sound as the most important to humans, and replied, "Ears." But the mother enlightened him with the right answer....

That was a wrong answer. After a while, she asked the same question to her son, who replied, "Our eyes, as sight is important to everybody." The answer was not correct. A few years later, her husband died and she cried placing her head on the shoulder of her young son, who was an adult by then.

She then asked the same question to her son, with tears rolling down her eyes. The son was very much surprised to hear that question on that sad occasion and he looked confused. The mother then told him, "The most important part of the body is the shoulder." He said: "Because it can hold the head." She said, "No, it is because it can hold the head of a grieving person or loved one when they cry. Son, in life, a time comes when everyone needs a shoulder to cry on."

It means one should be sympathetic to the pain of others, who will never forget your sympathy.

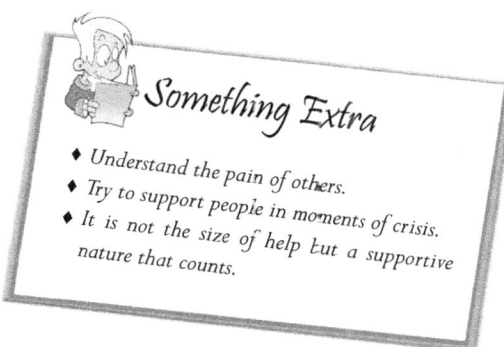

Something Extra

- Understand the pain of others.
- Try to support people in moments of crisis.
- It is not the size of help but a supportive nature that counts.

The Real Peace

Staying Calm amidst Turbulence is a Sign of Strength!

A King announced a hefty prize to an artist, who would paint the best picture of peace. Many artists tried their luck. But the outcome was interesting…

The King saw their pictures but shortlisted only two – one was that of a calm lake with peaceful towering hills around it and a blue sky full of

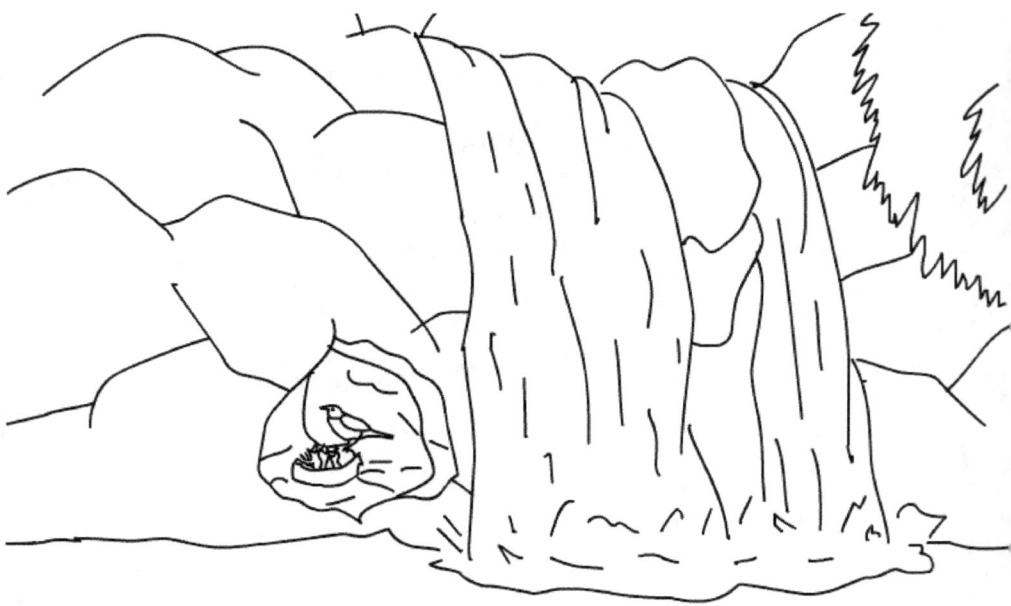

white clouds, overhead. The lake looked like a perfect mirror of peaceful surroundings.

The other picture also had mountains which were dry and rugged, with a turbulent sky overhead, lashing lightning and rain. A waterfall was making lot of noise down the mountainside. It was all a noisy scene. But, behind the waterfall was a rack with a small crack and inside it was a tiny bush. Inside the bush was a small mother bird, who built a nest and sat peacefully, unaware of the angry sky, noisy waterfall or disturbing environment. This presented a perfect picture of peace!

The King chose the second picture for prize! For him, peace meant staying calm at heart amidst all noises. It was the real meaning of PEACE — *the peace within*.

Something Extra

- Peace is not grave like silence.
- Staying calm amidst din is a sign of strength.
- Move along with the world and never run away from it.

Thoughts of Kabir

Thoughts and words of great men always inspire us!

Kabir was a saint and one of India's greatest spiritual thinkers. As a social reformer, he tried to uplift the downtrodden and preached against useless religious rituals. He also tried to reconcile religious differences and advocated love and unity among all classes of society laying stress on honest, simple and spiritual life. He showed them the path of worship and salvation, and urged to shun orthodox practices and superstitions. Kabir expressed his thoughts in simple language and addressed the common man. Some of his profound thoughts are mentioned below for the benefit of the reader:-

When the body is burnt, it becomes ash
When it is not burnt, worms eat it up.
A soft clay vessel will break,
When water is poured into it
Such is the nature of the body.
Why, oh brother, just then puffing and blowing thyself out?
As the bee collects honey with great nest
So the fool collects wealth

When a man is dead, they say,
'Take him away! Take him away!
Why allow a ghost to remain?'
His wedded wife accompanies him to the door,
and after that his male friends
All other members of his family,
go up till the cremation ground,
The soul departs all alone.

Who is a Hindu? Who is a Turk?
Both inhabit the same earth
One reads the Vedas, the other the Quran.
One is a Maulana, the other a Pandit.
They are like earthen vessels,
Having different names but made of the same earth.
Both are misled and have not found God.
The external forces conceal from our eyes the deep meaning of existence,
True faith resides in the heart.

Long not for a dwelling in heaven,
And fear not to dwell in hell,
What will be, will be,
O my soul, hope not at all
Sing the praises of God
From whom the supreme reward is obtained.

Be not glad at the sight of prosperity,
And grieve not at the sight of adversity:
As is prosperity, so is adversity;
What God proposes shall be accomplished.

Some of Kabir's *dohas* in Hindi follows:-
Jahaan dayaa, wahaan dharm hai,
Jahaan lobh, tahaan paap
Jahaan krodh, wahan kaal hai,
Jahaan krishana, tahan aap.

It means kindness is the basis of true religion; greed is a sin and anger is the cause of destruction. Kabir says, to forgive is divine. In the following *doha*, Kabir advises us to cultivate humility:-

Kabira garv na keejiye, kaal gahe kar kes
Na jaane kit mare hai, kyaa des kyaa pardesh.

Do not nurture pride, as one does not know when and where one is destined to die.

In another *doha*, Kabir advises not to postpone one's work, as one does not know what will happen in the next moment:-
Kaal kare so aaj kar, aaj kare so aab
Pal main parley hojagi, bahuri karega kab.

Kabir advises against worry in the following *doha*:-
Chintaa aise daakini, kaat kalejaa khaaye
Baid heelaraa kija karey, kalan tak dava lagaay.

Worry is a silent killer and no medicine can cure it.

His masterpiece and popular *doha* is:-
Kabira khadaa bazaar main, maange sabki khair
Na kohon si dosti, no kohon se bair.

Kabir wishes welfare of all; he is neither friend nor foe to anybody.

In another *doha*, saint Kabir advises self-analysis and not to find faults in others. He says:-
Bura jo dekhan main chala
Bura na milia koye
Jo dil khoja aapna,
Mujsa bura na koye.

'When I went to find a bad person, I could not find any. However, when I looked within me, I thought no one was worse than me!' Thus we need not find faults in others, but look within ourselves and remove our own faults. In another *doha*, kabir points towards the insecurity and miseries of life and says:-

Chalti chakki dekh ke,
Diya kabira roye
Do patun kek beach main,
Sabut bacha na koye.

It means that nothing remains intact between the two grinding stones; life is all full of insecurity and miseries.

Aise vaani boliye,
Man ka aapa khoye,
Aapan ko sheetal kare,
Auron ko sukhe deye.

In this *doha*, Kabir advises us to speak gently without pride, ego and hatred. A sweet tongue not only calms our nerves, but gives a soothing effect to the listener.

Kabir gives a formula for leading a pure, peaceful life in the following *doha*:

Kabira man nirmal bhaya,
Jaisey ganga neera
Pachhey pachhey Hari phirey
Kahat Kabira Kabira

A simple and pure life without malice for any one keeps the mind clean and humble. In this pure state, God will always be with you.

Something Extra

- A word is priceless if one knows how to use it.
- Never put off your work till tomorrow what you can do today.
- Have patience; everything comes out in time.

The Wanderers

The nobler the blood, the less the pride

Two wanderers met on the sea beach. They had a friendly talk. One said to the other,

"At the high tide of the sea, long ago,
With the point of my staff,
I wrote a line, upon the sand

Which the people still pause to read
And they are careful
That none shall erase it!"

The other man said, "I too wrote a line upon the sand, but it was at low tide, and the waves of the sea washed it away. But tell me, what did you write?"

And the first man said, "I wrote, as follows:

I am he who is....

Now tell me what did you write?"

And the other man answered, I wrote this, "I am but a drop of the great ocean."

—KHALIL GIBRAN

Something Extra

- Try to be humble.
- Self-praise is of no use.
- Greatness lies when others praise you.

Thank God - For Your Blessings

The Secret of True Happiness!

Most of us in this material world do not count the blessings in our life and mourn only about the losses. Is there a good way to be more positive in life?

The important thing is to count on our blessings and thank God for what he has given us, and convert the losses into gains. God has given us numerous blessings and CONTENTMENT is the top of all. It all depends on our mental attitude and how we react to the happenings in our life. The following two lives provide some guidance:-

"Two men looked out of the prison bars,
One saw the mud, the other saw stars."

This is how the right attitude makes a difference! We must enjoy the good things which happen to us and be grateful to our creator instead of grumbling about unsavoury and sad things. It will be relevant to quote great poet GOETHE in the following lines:

"My crown is in my heart, not on my head;
Not decked with diamonds and Indian stones;
Not to be seen, my crown is called CONTENT.
A crown it is that seldom kings enjoy."

These lines nicely indicate the value of contentment. We may, briefly, mention our many blessings in life, which are common to most of us, as follows:

1. Our body and good health
2. The house where we live
3. Our life partner
4. The children
5. Free air that we breathe and without which we cannot live and the life standing water and sunshine.
6. Our food and clothing
7. Good company and good friends and relatives
8. The forests, the green grass and plants
9. The starry blue sky at night
10. The clouds, the rain which brings life and joy
11. The change in seasons
12. All good opportunities in our life
13. Faith, hope and courage and all good qualities which make life noble and nice
14. The peace of mind and inner strength

We should count these blessings and many more, and thank God for his love and kindness.

Something Extra

- Observe the world.
- Thank the faculties and opportunities given by God.
- Utilise them properly and prosper.

A Fight Against All Odds

Tales of Heroes can do wonders in moments of distress!

This is the story of a brave woman, who fought all odds and bounced back to life. It was an accident which nearly made her immobile for a couple of years. But she recovered. How?

It was possible only because of her determination and the loving care of her parents. Their motto was, "It does not matter what happens

to you. What really matters is how you react to it." This was her earliest lesson in survival.

A few years later, as a result of a freak incident at an office party, she was hospitalised on the ground of permanent hearing loss. In the hospital, she could see doctors and nurses talking, but could not hear their voices. In spite of all sorts of treatment and medication, there was no cure. But she had received great support from the hospital staff, parents and relatives. She had learnt from her voracious reading as to how brave people had overcome great challenges in life including disabilities, with grit and determination.

She fought her battle hard, drawing inspiration from the stories she read. With the help of sophisticated hearing aids and help extended by colleagues along with the loving care received from parents, she got back to work and started doing well. What an amazing success story!

Something Extra
- Never give up hope.
- Anyone can Fall in life.
- Rising from a Fall is indeed heroic.

Tit For Tat - A Lesson For Life

Ungrateful behaviour precedes untold miseries!

This is the story of an aged person, who was maltreated by his young sons. In our modern age, youngsters consider their elderly parents as great nuisance and grown up children often try to ignore them. A bitter father, who was at the receiving end of such a humiliation decided to give a fitting reply to his selfish sons. What was his plan?...

A retired person spent all his savings to build a big house. He had wife and three young sons. He gave one floor each to his sons, and lived with his eldest son at the ground floor, along with his wife. A few years

later, his wife expired and he became totally dependent on his eldest son for his food and daily needs. One day, this son complained that his other two brothers were not contributing to the upkeep of their father. So it was decided that the father would stay with each family, turn by turn, for an equal period. But this arrangement did not work out and the helpless father started taking his meals at a nearby *dhaba*.

This was not a satisfactory arrangement for the father. His old friends, realising his plight hatched a plan to teach a lesson to his sons who ill-treated their father. One day the father called his three sons and gave them tickets for a fully paid holiday for a month. They were very happy to accept this offer and went on a vacation with their families. When they returned, they found a builder in their house, who asked the sons to take away their belongings and vacate the house as it had been sold to him by their father. They were also shocked to know that their father had left for an unknown destination without leaving any contact address. This was the fitting reply the old father gave to his sons for the maltreatment and humiliation heaped on him!

Human beings make the mistake of becoming too attached to their family and worldly possessions. They come to grief when they feel rejected by their own people. It is therefore, essential to train our minds in spiritual pursuits and develop an affinity towards God, so that we do not feel lonely and neglected in the old age. Sri Ramakrishna said, "The best way to live life is to live like a caretaker. A caretaker does not maintain any attachment for his possessions and remains calm even if they are snatched away from him."

Something Extra

- Inculcate good moral values in children.
- Children need to be made self-reliant.
- Problems must be solved through dialogues.

Forty Years Together

The heart that truly loves never forgets!

A husband and wife had a long married life. One night, the wife found her husband missing from their bed. She got up to look for him and found him sitting in the dining room with moist eyes. She watched him and said, "Dear, what is the matter? What are you doing here?"

The husband said, "Do you remember when we were dating 40 years ago?" The wife, touched by her husband's concern said. "Yes, I remember. I was only 18 then."

The husband then said haltingly, "Do you remember when your father caught us making love behind the couch? The wife came closer and said, "Yes, I remember." The husband then said, "Do you remember how he pointed his revolver on my face and shouted, "Either you marry my daughter or be ready to go to jail for 40 years." His wife replied very gently, "Yes, I remember all that." Then the man, wiping tears from his cheeks said, "If that happened, I would have got out today!"

Something Extra

- There are certain memories which can never be erased from our minds.
- One always remembers his first love.
- If one is married for long, there develops an inseparable bond or companionship.

Lost to Win

Sacrifice is a jewel that will shine throughout a life time and beyond!

This is the story of an ace sportsman--a table tennis player, who won a match but got himself declared as a loser in order to help another needy player to get a job. But that does not put full stop to his success...

A sportsman applied for the post of an engineer and as per rules, he had to win a match against others to qualify. When he won the match, the referee came to him and made him agree to be declared as a loser as his opponent needed that job badly, in view of his adverse financial condition. He had to support his mother, sisters and younger brother, and his father had expired a week ago. This sportsman who sacrificed his job in favour of another person soon got another good job. There he worked hard and rose high in the career after getting quick promotions. He also won all India championships for his company and brought honour for himself.

By losing the winnable match to favour a needier person for a job, this sportsman showed his large-heartedness. This kind gesture further reinforced his success and prosperity in later life in another well-deserved manner!

Something Extra
- For the deserving, opportunity is never a problem.
- A small favour to the needy returns as a mega opportunity later.
- Always try to diversify and avoid stagnation.

The Great Illusion

Dangers of self-love and illusions of true love!

A Guru had a disciple who was a householder. He used to advise his disciple to renounce the world and join him to attain the highest goal in life. The disciple was reticent. See how the Guru played an interesting episode in his life...

The disciple used to say, "Sir, how can I leave my affectionate parents, loving wife and children?" The Guru said, "All these are mere illusion. I will show you the reality." The Guru then gave a pill to the disciple to swallow. After taking the pill, the disciple became still like a corpse but did not lose his consciousness.

Following this development, the members of the disciple's house were overcomed by grief and all were wailing. Hearing the loud cries, a holy man appeared on the scene, who saw the dead body and touched it. Then he said, "I have a medicine which can bring him back to life. But another person has to die in his place." Surprisingly, for the young man, nobody was ready to die and all the relatives excused themselves on some pretext or another. The affectionate parents said, "We have to look after the big household." The loving wife said, "I have to look after my small children." The disciple was hearing everything and he got up suddenly and touched the feet of the holy man, who was none else, but his Guru. The disciple then said, "Sir, I will follow you. Let us go."

Something Extra

- Material life develops bonding with material things.
- Never overplay spiritual matters with real life.
- Take one path and stick to it.

Face of Humility

It is easy to find faults in others, but difficult to look for it within oneself!

A man, after realising that he was a great sinner, went to a holy person and said, "Sir, I am a great sinner. Please advise, as to how I can be saved. The holy man said, "Go and find out a greater sinner than you are, or bring something which is worse than you."

He went away, looked around, but could not find anything worse than him! Then a thought came to him, as he saw his own excrement

and said, "Surely, this is something worse than me." So he wanted to pick it up and take it to the holy man. As soon as he stretched his hands, he heard a voice from the rubbish "O sinner, how come you think me worse than you." I was a delicious pudding pleasing to all. Due to my misfortune, I was reduced to this horrible condition, when you ate me up. So do not touch me again for further degradation!" Hearing this, the man learnt a lesson in true humility and attained the highest stage of perfection.

Something Extra

- One should not always look for other's mistakes.
- One must first try to rectify or improve oneself.
- One should never think that one is perfect.

Practical Lesson

A Good Leader always leads from the front!

This is an interesting story of a school principal who literally tried to lead the students by examples. He demonstrated how not to waste food. What did he do to send his message that was loud and clear!

One day, he visited the hostel mess, where the students had just finished their lunch. There, he was shocked to see a lot of leftover food

in several plates lying on the table. He called up all the students and in their presence, ate the leftover food from one plate. Then he gave a pep talk about the food shortage and the starving millions, below the poverty line, in our country. He impressed upon the students to take as much food in their plates, as they actually needed and not to waste any food. The above practical lesson of the principal had a great effect on the students, who took the vow in his presence, not to waste any food, in the future.

Something Extra

- Hollow preaching is useless.
- Leading by example makes an impact.
- A good lesson from a good teacher remains in our minds for a lifetime.

Consequence of Fear

A brave man dies only once but a coward dies a million times!

A philosopher was walking in a garden and felt something following him. When he looked back, there was none but a shadow. It was death!

The philosopher questioned the shadow: "Who are you and where

are you going?" The shadow muttered: "I am the spectre of death and I am going to fetch a hundred dead bodies." Saying this, it disappeared.

Next day, that place was hit by plague and a thousand people died. The same philosopher, while walking in the garden met the shadow of death and asked, "You told me that you were going to fetch a hundred dead bodies, but in the town one thousand people have died. How do you explain this?"

Death replied, "That is not my fault. I got only one hundred persons, but the nine hundred died only out of fear of dying!"

This is the result of fear. We should not lose our confidence and live life without fear.

Something Extra

- Fear comes out of ignorance.
- Cure ignorance with more and more knowledge.
- Confront anxiety with focussed actions.

Unnesessary Worry

Live in the moment and be happy!

A rich man amassed so much of wealth that another seven generations could enjoy it. Still he was unhappy and had a worried look. Subsequently, he fell ill. On being quizzed by his wife, the man finally revealed his cause of worry. What was it?

His wife asked him, "Your illness is due to your worry. Please tell me, what makes you worry? You have everything and there is hardly any reason for your anxiety." The rich man thought for a while and said, 'Yes I have everything and much more so that our seven generations can live on that." His wife intervened to say, "Then, what is bothering you?" he said, "Oh, but I am worried about the 8th generation?!"

This is a glaring example of unnecessary worry. We should take care of our present and need not worry much spoiling our future.

Something Extra

- Never worry about things not in our control.
- Farsightedness is fine, but overdoing it is nonsense.
- Money need not always give security and mental peace.

A Story of Broken Trust

Chicanery Gets Hard Lashing!

A famous Sufi saint set out on a long journey accompanied by his disciples. When they were feeling tired and hungry, they took rest under the shade of a tree which had a bunch of birds perched on its branches. Then the animal instincts of one of his disciples worked and that led to an unpleasant situation…

One of the disciples of the saint took out his bow and arrow and killed one bird as a supplement to their food. At this, other birds started croaking and making noise which attracted the attention of the Sufi, who, using his spiritual powers, talked to the leader of the birds and enquired the reason for their unusual croaking. The head bird said they wanted justice for the killing of one of their team-mates. The Sufi pulled up the disciple and asked for an explanation for his cruel act. The disciple tried to excuse himself saying that he committed no offence as hunting was permitted. The head bird reacted by saying, "As Sufis are harmless people, we were not scared. If you were common people, we would have flown away, so you have deceived us."

The Sufis thought over this and agreed that even though hunting was allowed, the disciple had broken the trust of these unsuspecting birds. The accused was, therefore adjudged guilty and given a severe punishment.

Something Extra

- Never betray trust.
- Never resort to violence thinking the victim is weak.
- Never act on the basis of loopholes in the system.

How Little Things Matter

Even Small Steps make a Difference!

Once a man was walking along a beach and noticed another man repeatedly picking up something from the ground and throwing it into the sea. He decided to check it out.....

The man who was looking at this became curious and came closer to see what the other man was doing. He was actually picking up small

fish and hurling them into the sea. These fish had been washed ashore by the sea waves and could not go back to the sea water. He asked the other man why he was doing that. The other man replied, "I am throwing them back into the water to save them." The first man said, "Yes, I know, there are thousands of small fish on the beach. Throwing back a few would not make much difference."

That man smiled picking up another fish and throwing it back to the water and said, "This will surely make a difference at least to that one!"

And he was right. Even little things matter!

Something Extra

- Be positive on all your actions.
- Do not harp on big bang results for all your actions.
- An act must satisfy the doer, not necessarily the onlooker.

Unwanted Desires

Too much of pampering can play spoilsport!

A man had a pet dog, which he loved very much. The pampered dog in turn would play funny games and poke pranks at its master. Finally, the master decided to mend the ways of the pet dog in a novel way.

One day, a learned man came to his house and both sat down for a chat. All of a sudden the dog came and jumped into the lap of the master, licking his cheek. The visitor did not like it and expressed his displeasure to the house owner, and admonished him for pampering the dog so much. This had the desired result; the man decided to teach a lesson to the dog. Every time the dog would jump to lick his face, it was given a kick. The dog was quick to learn and changed its habit, improved and behaved well, thereafter.

Similarly, our unwanted desires are like a pampered pet trying to overwhelm us. Proper control in the form of repeated blows and counter thoughts can cure them.

Something Extra

- Wishes are like horses.
- Try to develop doable thoughts.
- Learn self-control and abandon unwanted desires.

Good and Bad Turns

Forget and forgive must be the philosophy of all good persons!

Two friends were walking through a desert. During the journey, they quarrelled over a dispute and one friend slapped the other. The one, who was slapped wrote on the sand, "Today my best friend slapped me." He was hurt, but did not say anything. His logic was edifying...

As they walked on, they came to an oasis, where they decided to take bath. Unfortunately, the one who got slapped, got stuck in the mud and was about to get drowned. However, the other saved him and brought him out of the pool. The person, who was saved, engraved on the stone "Today, my best friend saved my life." The other enquired, "When I hurt you, you wrote on sand. But now, when I saved you, you engraved it on the stone. Please explain this."

The other friend said: "When someone hurts you, you should forget it soon, like a writing on the sand gets blown away. But if someone does you good, try to remember it long, like the engraving on stone that cannot be blown away.

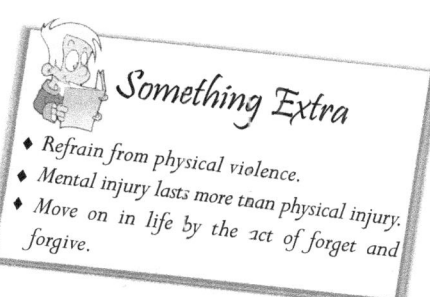

Something Extra
- Refrain from physical violence.
- Mental injury lasts more than physical injury.
- Move on in life by the act of forget and forgive.

Human Life is Precious

An elephant never knows its strength!

When a diamond merchant died, he bequeathed a rare and invaluable diamond to his wife. One day she sent out her younger son to the market to know and verify the market value of the diamond but advised him against selling it. He heard many prices from many merchants. Then…

First he took it to a vegetable seller, who offered some potatoes in exchange. Then he went to a shopkeeper, who offered a hundred rupees. Then he took it to a goldsmith, who valued it at two thousand rupees. A diamond merchant was prepared to give ten thousand rupees. At last he came to know about a man, who was an expert in rare and precious diamonds; so he asked his opinion. The man said that the diamond was worth many millions of rupees and was invaluable.

This story is an allegory of human life itself which is priceless. It depends how a person uses it and values it. Majority of human beings do not realise the true value of life and waste it in useless pursuits. Human life is priceless; it is a rare gift from the God. It should he used properly to realise its best possible value by focussing on noble causes.

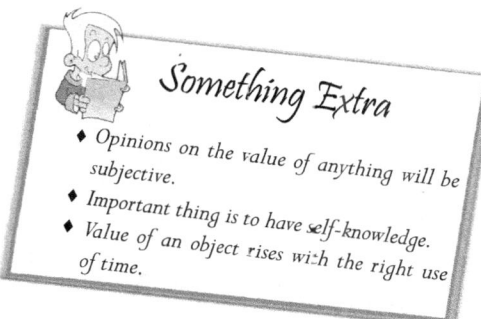

Something Extra

- Opinions on the value of anything will be subjective.
- Important thing is to have self-knowledge.
- Value of an object rises with the right use of time.

Acceptance of Existence

Accepting God in broad humility!

This is the story of a Sufi mystic by the name, Junnaid who would express his gratitude to God for his existence, and the love, care and compassion bestowed on him. Once Junnaid and his companions set out on a journey and they starved without food for three days continuously. The outcome was a lesson to all...

They did not get any food and water from the villages they crossed. Thinking that his teachings were bad and selfish, the villagers shunned him and refused to help. On the third day, Junnaid and his followers were in great trouble. His disciples began to murmur and said, "Now let us see how he expresses his gratitude for his existence and what does he say in his prayers?"

When the time of prayers came, Junnaid said his prayers as usual, expressing deep gratitude to the God. After the prayer, the disciples started grumbling and said: "This is not tolerable. We have been suffering from thirst and hunger for the last three days! We have not even slept and all are tired. Here you are still thanking God for your existence and telling that it takes care and is very compassionate!"

Junnaid heard this and said: "My prayer does not depend on any condition which is of ordinary nature. Whether I get food or not, I won't blame my existence. They are only small things in this vast universe. It won't matter to me if I don't get food and water and even if I die. I will pray in the same manner. It hardly makes any difference to this vast universe whether Junnaid is dead or alive!"

The above story shows how life should be accepted by all. Life is not obliged to fulfil all our desires; it gives us what we deserve. Acceptance of life as it is will give us satisfaction and happiness. For a truly religious person, acceptance of whatever life brings is real PRAYER!

Something Extra

- Prayers are not the time for complaining. Convert your Prayers as Thanks Giving.
- No true believer will blame God for small discomforts.

The Value of Truth

One more experiment with truth!

About 1000 years ago, in Iraq, there was a child named Abdul Qadir. One day he heard a voice urging him to undertake his greatest mission in life. He felt inspired and told his mother that he wanted to go to Baghdad to pursue higher education. The mother agreed and gave him an important advice...

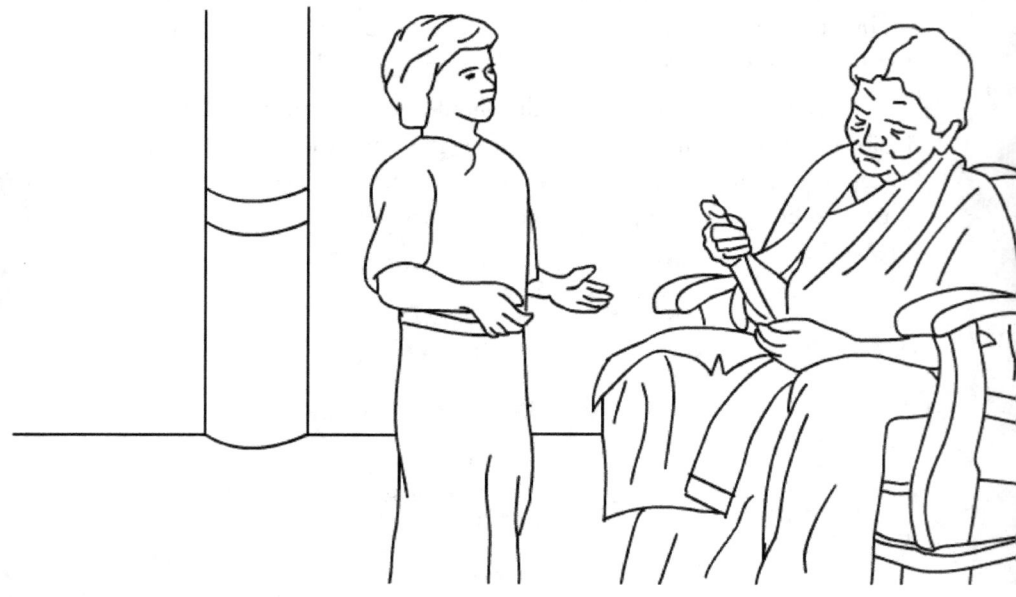

She granted him permission to go, but stitched 40 gold coins inside his coat's lining, and said. "Oh, my son, since you are going, I shall bear the separation from you for the service of God. But do follow my advice--always feel the truth, speak the truth and propagate the truth, even at the risk of your life."

Qadir heard his mother carefully and promised to follow her advice; Come what may! On the way to Baghdad, he was attacked by robbers. He honestly told them about the gold coins hidden in his coat. When the robbers found them, the robbers were astonished and the leader asked Qadir what prompted him to reveal the hidden treasure. Qadir said: "My mother had advised me to speak the truth even at the risk of my life. I promised her to follow her advice. That is why I told you the truth." The robbers were impressed by his sincerity and felt remorseful from that day onwards and gave up robbing people and began a good life, afresh.

That small child was only eight years old when he left home to pursue knowledge and later became a great saint, who was known as Sheikh Abdul Qadir Gelani. He followed his mother's advice; practised truth and became a saintly scholar and social reformer.

It is said that Truth is God or God is truth. We should always live by the truth.

Something Extra

- Never compromise on educational opportunities.
- Never stop a person from achieving his inner calling.
- Consequences of honesty are worth fighting.

The Great President

A Noble Soul never ceases to delight and comfort!

During the American civil war, Abraham Lincoln, the famous President of the U.S.A. visited hospitals to cheer the injured soldiers. Thus he came across an injured soldier, who was on his death bed. The President asked him, "Is there anything I can do for you?" He had a curious request....

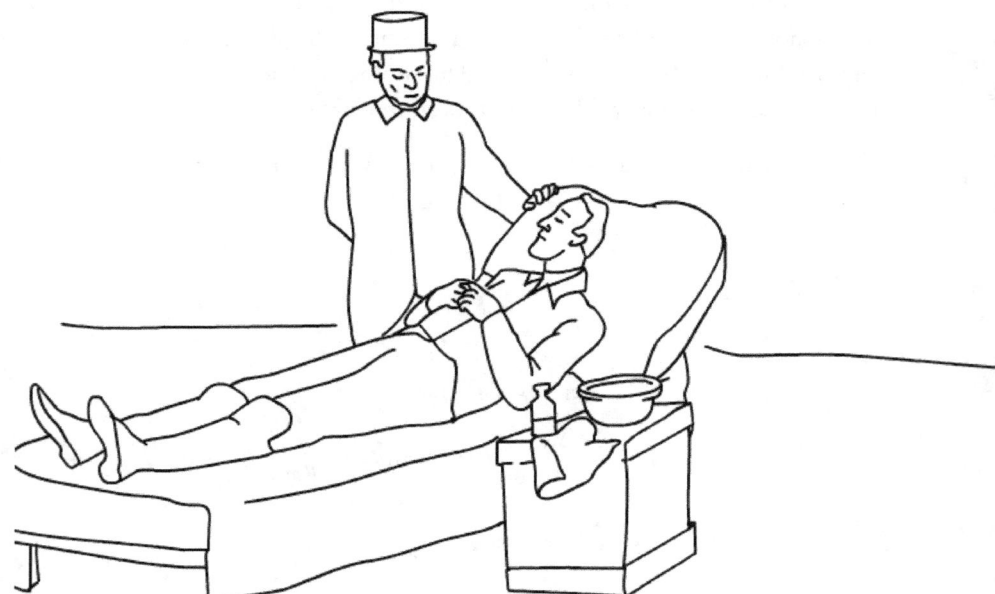

The soldier, without knowing the identity of the visitor, said, "Please write a letter to my old mother." The President sat beside him to take the dictation. The soldier said, "Dear mother, I have been fatally injured, while fighting for my country and shall die shortly. Do not grieve for me. May God bless you." Lincoln closed the letter with a postscript "written for your son by Abraham Lincoln." When the soldier saw the letter, he was greatly astonished that his visitor was none else but the President himself. Lincoln again enquired, "Is there anything else, I can do for you?" The young man said, "Please hold my hand so that I can die peacefully."

The kind President obliged and the soldier died in peace. Even small compassionate deeds matter a great deal.

Something Extra
- Acknowledge the good acts of every person.
- Stand by your team in moments of crisis.
- Fill your life with acts of heroism and less of regrets.

The Positive View

A nightmare named debt!

A man was in heavy debt and very disturbed that he could not sleep at night because of financial burden. Deep in depression, he decided to end his life, but shared his problem with one of his close friends. The friend listened to him patiently and looked for a solution. What was the friend's game plan?

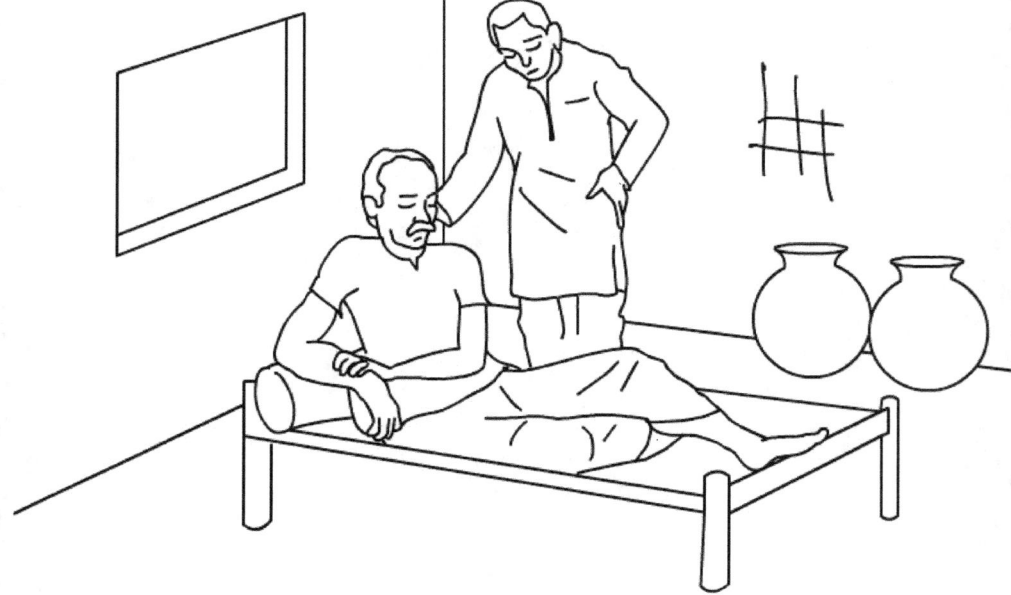

As soon as the man finished his words, his friend asked him about the assets he possessed in terms of money and property. He did not talk anything about the debt. The man was surprised and became conscious of the fact that he possessed so many things. He had a house, agricultural land, lot of grain in his store and several cattle besides many friends and well wishers.

The situation changed entirely. He then had no worries about the debt and realised that he had enough resources and there was no cause for anxiety. He became cheerful and was full of confidence that he can solve his problem. All this happened because of the positive view expressed by the friend who showed him the right way.

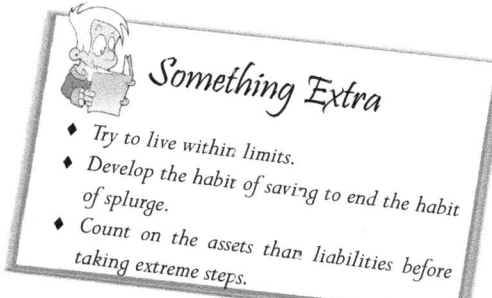

Something Extra

- Try to live within limits.
- Develop the habit of saving to end the habit of splurge.
- Count on the assets than liabilities before taking extreme steps.

Encouragement Leads to Success

When one door closes many other doors will open automatically!

A word of encouragement can often lead to success. This is the success story of Nathaniel Hawthorne – one of the greatest names in American literature. What transpired in his later life?

When he lost his job, he came home heartbroken to tell the news to his wife. But she surprised him with an exclamation of joy, saying "Now you can write your book." He said, "But what shall we live with, when I am writing this book." His wife opened a drawer and brought out a lot of money. He asked: "Where did you get all this money?" She replied, "I always knew that you are a genius. So I kept saving whatever you used to give me for housekeeping. So this money is enough to keep us going for the whole year."

As a result of her encouragement and trust in her husband's ability, Hawthorne produced one of the greatest novels of American literature.

Something Extra

- Creative people can never be crushed.
- They must dig deep and discover gold with their talents.
- Never lose heart by one lost opportunity.
- Assume the best is yet to come.

Curious Questions - Right Answers

Turning puzzles into delightful embarrassments!

A King asked his minister three puzzling questions and asked him to find answers. What were the questions and what were the answers."

The questions were the following:-

1. What is that which you give here for which you get a reward here?
2. What is that which you give here for which you get a reward there?
3. What is that which you give here and for which you get a reward neither here nor there?

The minister said: "Your majesty, please give me Rs 30,000/- and I shall give you answers after a week." The King gave him the money. After a week, the minister beseeched the King, "Sir, I deposited Rs 10,000/- in a bank, in your account. I have given it here and you will be rewarded with interest here, anytime you want. This answers your first question." He continued to say "Sir, I purchased food for Rs 10,000/- and distributed it among the poor and the needy. This was done with your money, on your behalf. You have given this money here for which you will be rewarded in the next birth. This answers your second question." The minister added further, "The balance Rs 10,000/- I wasted on wild pursuits, wine, women, dances, etc. For all these, you will be rewarded neither here, nor there. This answers your third question." The King was satisfied with the three answers and rewarded the minister.

Something Extra

- There are many ways to spend money.
- Put money in savings for future gains.
- Spend on charity for bliss in afterlife.
- Money spent on utter pleasure is waste and useless.

A Legend from the Puranas

Keeping Busy is a positive way to deflect negative thoughts and feelings!

A man had lot of work and he felt tired and unhappy at the end of the day. He was a devotee of Lord Shiva, so he invoked Lord Shiva's help. Lord Shiva appeared before him and he pleaded: "Lord, please send me someone who can carry out my orders whatsoever.'

Lord Shiva granted his wish and sent *Betaal* to do the needful. But there was a condition attached to it. He should never keep the *Betaal* without work, otherwise he would kill the man.

The man was much pleased and he got many things done every day.

One day, he had no work for the *Betaal* and he realised that without work, the *Betaal* would kill him. So he asked *Betaal* to erect a pillar which he did. Then he told him to climb to the top and then come down and then keep repeating this process. Thus, the *Betaal* was kept occupied endlessly.

In this story, there is lesson that our mind is like the *Betaal*. It should always he kept busy in doing something productive, otherwise an idle mind becomes a devil's workshop.

Something Extra
- Never sit idle.
- Engage in a useful activity.
- Busy mind helps to keep a positive outlook.

Different Perspectives

Seeing the Big Picture in a Hard Way!

A man had four sons. When they grew up as adults, he wanted to teach them on how to judge things properly and not superficially. He sent them on errands, turn by turn, to go and see a fig tree, in different seasons. What was the result?

The first one went in the winter and reported that the tree had a bent and looked ugly. The second one went in the spring and found it all green and full of buds. The third son went in the summer and said it was full of blossoms, smelt sweet and looked beautiful. The fourth son, who went during the 'autumn' had an entirely different view. He said the tree was bearing fruits and full of life and fulfilment. Thus, all the four sons saw the same tree in different seasons and derived different perspectives of the same thing. The father then told them that while each one was correct in his own way, yet no one got the complete picture of the tree.

In the same manner, we humans view our lives in different ways in different circumstances. In difficulty, we cry and feel sad; we laugh in good times and become angry when frustrated. A mature, wise person will judge life in totality and will arrive at a balanced view of life.

Something Extra
- Do not accept any judgement as final.
- Perspectives do not stand for reality.
- Look at things in its totality.

An Astrologer's Dilemma

False Sense of Greatness can Crumble in a second!

A lady was travelling by train from Delhi to Agra. A man seated next to her was an astrologer, who was going to Agra to meet his clients for whom he had given appointments. He was a well known astrologer. He would not only forecast the destiny, but also suggest means to improve or even cure bad things.

During the journey, he had been confirming his appointments on the cell phone and had busy schedules for the whole day. But suddenly, the train came to a halt midway between Mathura and Agra due to a mechanical fault and there was no early hope of resumption of the journey. The astrologer became desperate as there was no way he could meet his clients. His cell phone also stopped working due to failure in the battery. Finally, he had to borrow the cell phone from the lady, who reluctantly obliged him and was amused to see his predicament. On the cell phone, he asked his agent at Agra to cancel all his appointments due to this inconvenience. His clients were all angry and began shouting at the agent, as it could be made out from their voices on the cell phone. It was a pity that an astrologer who could forecast the destiny of his clients could not forecast his own destiny!

Something Extra

- Do not be so crazy about knowing the future.
- Knowledge that does not help oneself will not benefit others.
- Always have a crisis management plan.

A Story of Love and Service

Service to the mankind is the best form of worship!

Many years ago, there was a pious man who led a good, cosy life but lacked satisfaction in life. He wanted to discover the reason and define its real purpose. Did he get answers!.....

One day he renounced his house and went to the Himalayas to seek enlightenment. After prolonged penance, he came to the conclusion that his soul was divine and God was within. He felt elated at the realisation, and started back to the plains after leaving his Himalayan abode.

On his way back, he saw a beautiful temple. Since he was tired, he came close to it but found its door closed. He knocked the door and a voice asked, "Who are you?" He replied, "I am a devotee, who has realised God." The voice within said, "Go away, my temple cannot have two of us."

The man went back to the Himalayas again to seek more penance. After a long process of self-enquiry and inner exploration, he came back to the same temple again and knocked at the closed door. The voice within again enquired, "Who are you?" The man replied, "I am same as you and none else." At this, the door opened and the man entered and became one with the presiding deity, in deep meditation. After a long period of time, the man grew bored inside the stone image. He therefore, came out of it, left the temple and mingled with the common people.

He sought the company of all and sundry. He loved everybody; served the needy and the helpless; and consoled them in their miseries sharing their joys and sorrows. In doing so, he drew boundless satisfaction and discovered the true meaning of existence in love and selfless service.

One day, the man happened to pass by the same temple and found its door open. The voice from within said, "Come inside, I will give you liberation and freedom from all suffering." However, the man said: "Sorry, I can't accept your invitation. I have to work for my people and I can't leave them even for my own liberation." Then, all of a sudden, he experienced a flash of enlightenment which transformed his whole being. He found himself stretched in the vastness of the sky, moving all over the space, enjoying and mingling with the whole creation. This was a thrilling experience of his all-pervading existence in the infinite drama of creation.

Something Extra
- Be a part of the society you live.
- Try to be of use to your family and immediate society.
- The inner joy from helping others will destroy all dissatisfaction.

An Incident of True Religion

Small favours can deliver big satisfaction!

True religion is not all about the observance of rites and rituals. It lies in acts of kindness and compassion!

A man was walking on the road side, where heavy rainwater had flooded the road. There was nothing, but just water on the road and nothing else was visible. He was about to cross the road, when he saw

a car speeding towards him. He got scared, but the car slowed down as it came close to him and it stopped and allowed him to cross the road. Then the driver smiled at him waved and sped away. The driver of the car left a pleasant impression in the mind of the roadside traveller, who saluted him for his consideration and kind act.

In another case, a man, who, after finishing his job in an office failed to get any kind of transport to go to his hotel. Greatly upset, he stood on the road, alarmed at the sight of menacing dark clouds as it would rain any moment. Just then a gleaming big car pulled up beside him in front of the big house, where he was standing. The gentleman sitting on the wheel, sensing his distress, enquired about it. Knowing his problem, he asked the man to sit in his car and dropped him at his hotel. He then went back as the house where this man was standing belonged to the owner of the car. What an act of kindness even at the cost of personal inconvenience!

Something Extra
- Man is a social being.
- Try to sense the needs of others.
- Help someone with an act that can bring a smile on his/her face.

Another View of Life

Standing up for the poor and suffering amounts to service of the God!

A kind-hearted lady used to visit an *ashram* where orphans and street children were looked after well. One day the lady took her school-going daughter also with her. Her mother was always welcome there, but the daughter being new to the place felt bored. Then she saw three small girls huddled in a corner and looking terrified. Then...

A drunken man was seen abusing the girls and trying to take them away forcibly. The lady intervened and the man said: "These children are my relatives. Who are you to interfere?." The horrified girls ran to the lady for safety. The lady confronted the drunkard with courage and warned him to behave otherwise she would call the police. The man got scared and a compromise was worked out to leave the girls at the *ashram* in lieu of some monetary compensation, which was agreed to. After the settlement was reached, the bad man never disturbed the girls again. It was later discovered that the parents of these girls were murdered before the eyes of these children and this man, who was their uncle used to force them to do odd jobs and earn money which he would take away. This story shows how a kind lady helped those helpless girls and gave a new lease of life to them. This incident also gave a new perspective about life to the daughter of the kind-hearted woman, who also started going to the *ashram* and provide assistance to the inmates there.

Something Extra
- Never be scared to confront anti-socials.
- Never allow some one exploit our fears.
- Stand up for the cause of the poor and weak.

Strange But True!

Life is a sum total of many surprises!

Kanshi (name changed) was a poor labourer and he had a costly eye operation. He had no money to do it. But....

Kanshi, aged 58, lived with his wife and son. The latter worked in a factory and earned around Rs. 3000. The family struggled to meet the

two ends. Kanshi's wife also had to nurture her 3 year-old grandson as the daughter-in-law had ditched them.

Kanshi was suffering from a serious eye problem and was advised immediate operation at an eye hospital. At the hospital, he was told that the operation would cost around Rs. 20,000/. He came out of the hospital dejected as he could hardly afford the hospital expenses. He lost all hope and waited at the bus stop to go home. At that point of time, there came a rich, well-dressed person, from nowhere and asked Kanshi, "Hey, why are you looking so depressed?" Kanshi was surprised to see the stranger, but narrated his sad story. The kind stranger took him back to the hospital and fixed his operation, paying the advance amount. He also told Kanshi to come to the hospital the next day for operation. Kanshi was operated upon; and the stranger paid all the expenses and even arranged an auto to go home. Kanshi came home and the family was all wonder about the kind stranger who helped them benignly.

Is this real charity or a miracle!

Something Extra

- Surprising turnaround from difficult situations do happen.
- Never feel shy of sharing a difficulty with a person of concern.
- If something is destined to happen, it will happen.

Existence of God

Initiative is the key to accomplishment!

God is a mystery. Some people believe in God, some do not. This is a story about the existence of God.

A man went to a barber for a haircut, where he had a chat with the barber on God. The barber said: "I don't believe in God." The customer asked why he was a non-believer....

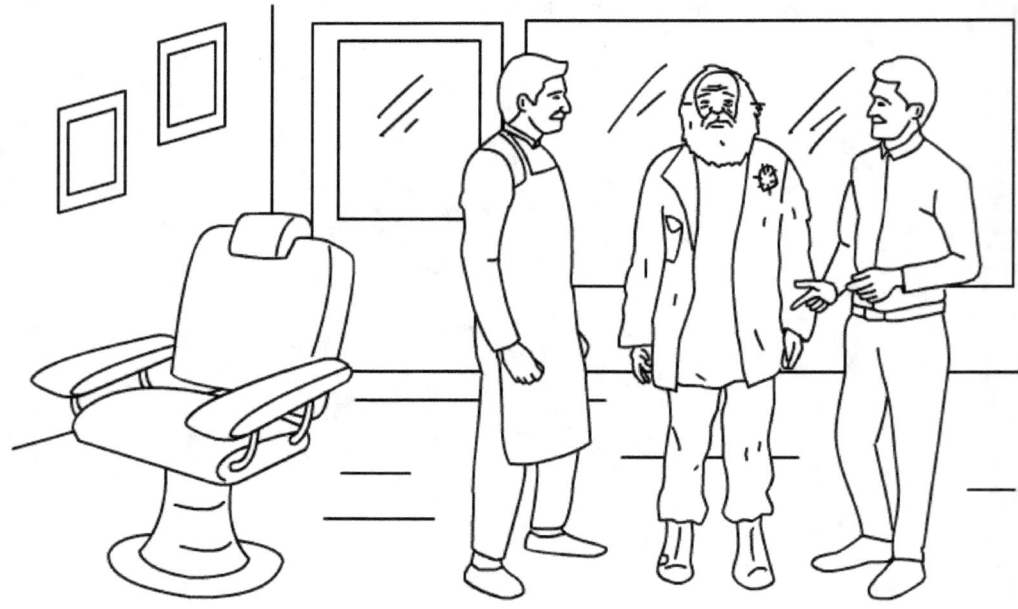

The barber replied, "You just go out in the street and see that you won't find God, anywhere." He further argued. "If God exists, why there is so much pain and suffering. A loving God should not allow this to happen. So I can't think that God exists."

The barber's argument made the customer think for a while and he did not want to enter into an unnecessary discussion, so he left the shop after the haircut. When he came out in the street, he found a dirty man with long unwashed hair and unshaven beard. He brought him to the barber's shop and said, "Look barbers do not exist." The barber said, "You can't say so, I am a barber standing before you so you can't say that barbers do not exist." The man said, "No, the barbers don't exist. If they existed, there would be no people with dirty long hair and untrimmed beard, like this man."

The barber said, "Oh, but barbers do exist. This man is so because he did not go to a barber." The customer chuckled to say. "Yes, that is the point. God too exists. That is what happens when people do not go to Him and do not seek His help. That is why, there is so much of pain and suffering. This story means that we can find God within us if we completely surrender to God. We cannot find him in the external world or see with our eyes. We have to feel and experience the existence of God for which we need to have full faith and devotion.

Something Extra
- Take initiatives and have faith in God.
- Nothing moves without taking the first step.
- Cynicism never takes any one very far.

G.B. Shaw and the Vegetarian Diet

Uncompromising Conviction differentiates heroes from the ordinary!

This is an interesting story from the life of famous writer G.B. Shaw, who was a staunch supporter of vegetarian diet. Did Shaw attempt to compromise?

When G.B. Shaw fell seriously ill, the doctors advised him to start taking meat, otherwise he would die. Being a strict vegetarian,

Shaw refused to heed that advice. The doctors again warned him of fatal consequences. However, Shaw dictated his will which read, as follows:-

"I solemnly declare that my coffin when carried to the graveyard, be accompanied by mourners of the following categories: first birds; second sheep, lambs and cows and other animals of the kind; third live fish from an aquarium. Each of these mourners should carry a placard bearing the inscription: O Lord, be gracious to our benefactor; G.B. Shaw, who gave his life for saving ours."

Some people eat meat because they think that it promotes physical strength. On the contrary, the elephant, the ox and the hare are known for their strength and physical capacity. It is, not at all necessary to eat meat as God has given us grains, vegetables, fruits, honey and milk which can easily meet our requirements of nutrition. There is absolutely no need for us to eat meat for which an innocent life has to be sacrificed.

Something Extra
- Be firm on your moral principles.
- Rise above situations that may compromise honour.
- Propagate any good cause to the larger public.

All for a Piece of Loin-Cloth

Invention is the mother of necessity!

Under instruction from his Guru, a disciple built a thatched hut away from the city and started living in it for doing his *sadhna* or spiritual exercise. Soon some incidents took place....

Every morning, after taking bath, he would spread his wet loin-cloth on a tree for drying. Then he would go to the neighbouring

village to beg food. One day, when he returned, he found his loin-cloth torn up by rats. So the villagers gave him a new one. After a few days, again the rats tore away the new piece, so he approached the villagers for a new one. The villagers advised him to keep a cat, which he did and the cat killed all the rats. Now the cat needed something to eat for survival. So the *sadhu* went to the village to beg some milk for her. The villagers then advised him to keep a cow so that he can get milk for the cat and avoid begging in the village. So he kept a cow, but the cow needed fodder to eat. The villagers again advised him to grow crops in the land around his hut, which he did. He had now enough crops, not only for the cow's fodder, but also for sale. So with the money so earned, he built a farmhouse and became a rich landlord, in due course. Consequently, he got married, established a household and was no longer a *sadhu*. He became a rich householder and lived like other worldly householders.

After long time, his Guru came to see him and was astonished to see his disciple living in this manner. So he enquired about it, "What is all this, my child?" The disciple felt ashamed and explained, "Sir, this was all for a single piece of loin-cloth."

This shows how ordinary folks get involved in their worldly activities in order to fulfil their desires.

Something Extra
- Never go for ad hoc solutions.
- Evolve solutions from one's own thinking and experiences.
- Maintain one's own identity.

The Story of Three Skulls

Knowledge that does not convert into Wisdom is Waste!

A King had three skulls and he asked the wisest man in his kingdom, as to which one was the best. To ascertain this, a test was conducted.....

The wise man took a rod and passed it through the ear of a skull. The rod came out of the second ear. Then he put the rod in an ear of

the second skull it came out of the mouth. When he inserted the rod in the ear of the third skull, it went right into the heart. The wise man recommended the third skull as the best.

The first skull belonged to those people, who hear words of wisdom through one ear and without thinking anything, let them out through the other ear. The second skull represented those people, who do not practise the wisdom so acquired, but is keen to preach it to others. Regarding the third skull, such people, after hearing wisdom, absorb it into their hearts and practise it in their real, daily lives.

Something Extra
- Develop a taste for knowledge.
- Absorb and retain that knowledge.
- Use that knowledge productively in real life too.

Detachment

Keeping the right distance is a part of safe driving!

A Jewish saint underwent persecution in Germany, under the Nazi regime. Without caring for the abuses on him, the saint bore the physical torture by detaching himself from his body and endured it as a silent spectator.

He practised a mental attitude of detachment which saved him even from death. Another person, in his place would have either died of torture or committed suicide. The practice of detachment helped him to service.

Detachment makes a person strong, but it has to be practised over a long period before one succeeds in acquiring such an attitude through will power and determination.

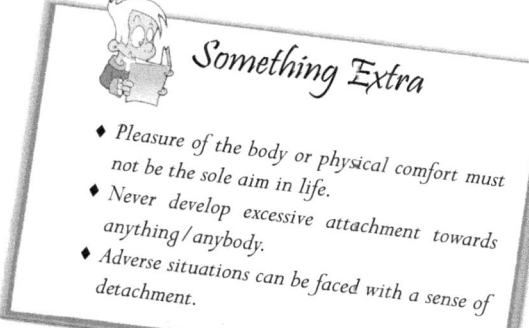

- Pleasure of the body or physical comfort must not be the sole aim in life.
- Never develop excessive attachment towards anything/anybody.
- Adverse situations can be faced with a sense of detachment.

Good News - Bad News

Never think money is for self-indulgence!

One day, a priest stood before the congregation and said: "I have both good news and bad news for you." The parish people were puzzled! They waited..

First the bad news, the priest said: "The church required a sum of US$1000 to repair the leaking roof. The repairs are urgent, otherwise the roof will fall down." At this the people groaned. Then the priest said, "Now the good news, enough money is available to carry out repairs, so there is nothing to worry." Everybody smiled and heaved a sigh of relief. The priest again said: "There is again some bad news and it is that the money is still in your pockets."

Something Extra

- Use money to build up your virtues.
- Spend a portion of money for the community.
- Unethical money can be a cause of tension too.

Daydreaming

The King of Fantasy World may not actually rule the kingdom!

One day a peasant went to a vegetable garden with the purpose of stealing some potatoes. He made some long-term plans in mind and his daydreaming went on. Finally....

He thought, "I will steal a sack full and sell it. With that money, I will buy a hen, who will lay eggs which will produce lots of chicken.

By selling the chicken, I will buy a cow which will give lots of milk. Then I will buy another cow and in this way, by selling more milk, I will buy more cows and open a dairy farm. I will not let anyone to steal my cows as I shall keep guard over them."

He was so much carried away with these thoughts that he forgot that he was in someone else's garden. Then there was some noise of a watchman coming. The man thought that a thief had come to steal in his farmhouse. So he shouted at the top of his voice. The watchman heard him and caught the peasant stealing and gave him a hard beating. That was the result of daydreaming.

Something Extra

- Live in the present and avoid fantasizing.
- Future is not in our control.
- Try and work hard to improve your present life.

A Jar of Life

Right priorities are crucial for Success!

A professor was teaching in a Philosophy class. He picked up an empty jar and filled it with golf balls. He then asked the students whether the jar was full and they agreed that it was. He was trying to explain a fact of life. What was it?

The professor then picked up some pebbles, put them into the jar and shook it. The pebbles rolled into the empty space between the golf

balls. He then asked the students again whether the jar was full, they agreed. Next, the professor took some sand and poured into the jar. The sand then spread into the empty space still left; he asked again if the jar was full. The students said yes.

The professor then took a glass of water and poured into the jar filling the empty space between the sand. The professor then said, "Now, I want you to imagine that this jar represents your life. The golf balls are the important things, like your family, friends and habits, etc. The pebbles represent other materials, possessions like house, job, car, etc. The sand represents everything else, the small stuff."

He further continued, "If you put the sand into the jar first, then no space will be left, for the pebbles and the golf balls. Likewise, if you spend all your time and energy on the small stuff of life, you will never have the time for important things."

In this way, the professor taught his students to pay more attention and give priority to the more important matters in life.

One student asked a question, "What was the role of water." The professor replied, "The water shows no matter how full your life may appear to be, there is always a scope for some improvement. You can always add something more useful to life."

Something Extra

- Perfection comes from continuous seeking.
- There is always scope for further improvement.
- Always look for options to grow and excel in life.

Promise of a Politician

Quick to promise and too quick to forget!

During election time, a politician undertook a tour of his constituency and asked people to vote for him. They asked, "What will you do for us, if we vote for you?" He had lot to promise....

"The politician thought for a while and said, "I will do something big for you, which no other politician can do." A clever voter questioned, "But what is that actually?" The politician, again thought for a moment and then blurted out, "I will build a bridge for you." He said this without knowing whether a bridge was needed or not!"

The puzzled people asked, "But we have no river here, so where is the need for a bridge?"

The politician replied, "Never mind, we will first make a river for you!"

How funny!

Something Extra
- Develop the spirit of questioning.
- Never fall for the lure of quick promises.
- Avoid those who insult intelligence and are foolish.

A Holy Man and the Humble Worm

Live life to the full!

Long ago, a sage was walking on a road, where hundreds of chariots passed daily. There he saw a worm furiously slithering away. He questioned it and got some amazing answers....

The sage asked the worm, "Why are you hurrying, what are you afraid of?" The worm replied, "I hear the noise of chariots which are drawing nearer. They will crush me. I must run and get out of the way. Sir life is precious and I won't like to die, if I can help. I don't want to go from the heaven of life to the hell of death." The sage said, "But you are only a worm! What do you know about joy and heaven in life! You should be happier as dead." The worm replied, "Sir in spite of what you say, living like as I am, I have got used to it. I may be a small worm but I have my own enjoyments. In my last life, I was a wealthy man but I performed wild misdeeds and now I am repenting for my follies. I am now doing penance."

The sage said, "Penance goes a long way. Since you have formed a mind now, you will achieve liberation one day. If you like, I can change your condition." The worm agreed. Soon a large chariot came and its wheel crushed the worm. Passing through several incarnations, the worm finally achieved liberation.

Something Extra

- Give dignity to all creatures.
- True remorse can wash away all regrets and sins.
- Always give the right guidance.

Love of God

Patience pays!

One day prophet Abraham, while sitting before his house, saw an old man walking with great difficulty, with the aid of a stick. Abraham asked him to take rest in his house and accept his hospitality for the day. Was it a sure proof of Abraham's kindness?...

The old man first declined, but upon persuasion by Abraham accepted his offer. The old man had his food and Abraham asked him to join him for prayer. He said, "I do not believe in God." At this Abraham got angry and turned him out of his house and went to sleep.

At night, Abraham had a dream in which God asked, "I sent you an old man to look after, what have you done with him?" Abraham replied, "God, that man was a non-believer, so I turned him away." God said, "I know that he does not believe in Me, but I have looked after him all this long, and you could not do that for one night." Abraham felt sorry, apologised to God and brought the old man back.

Something Extra
- Differences of opinion do not make another person an enemy.
- Be a good host and inculcate the habit of serving people.
- Do not give hope and then break it.

Marriage by Destiny or Default!

Sometimes even an onlooker gets the trophy!

A man fell in love with a girl and wanted to marry her. So he would write long letters to her, expressing his love. Did he marry her? Read on to find out……

After sending her dozens of letters, he came to meet her. To his dismay, the man discovered that the girl had fallen in love with the postman, the man who delivered her those letters and married him.

How strange! Is it marriage by destiny or default?

Something Extra
- A man of action is preferred over a man of imagination.
- Personal interaction is a must for the progress of any enterprise or relationship.
- Move on with a smile when a hurdle comes across.

How Wisdom Can Help?

The seat of knowledge is in the head of wisdom.

Emperor Jahangir was famous for his upright dispensing of justice. One day, his servant was pouring wine in the emperor's cup. Accidentally, or drop of wine fell on the King's robe. Greatly annoyed, Jahangir sentenced him to death. But the servant was unfazed...

The servant remained unperturbed and without hesitation, he poured the entire cup of wine over the king. This made Jahangir even angrier and he shouted; "Why did you do this even after hearing the death sentence?"

The servant replied, "Your majesty, you are renowned for your justice. Just think, after my death, people would rebuke you for giving me death sentence just because a drop of wine fell on you, by mistake! I did not relish the thought that your fame for justice might be thus maligned. I therefore, poured the whole cup on you so that justice appeared justified!"

The emperor was pleased, and he pardoned his servant and also rewarded him with money and promotion.

This is how wisdom can save even in great crisis.

Something Extra
- Never react whimsically to any situation.
- Face even the harshest comment with a smile.
- Politely assuage the feelings of the aggrieved party.

Author: Prof. Shrikant Prasoon
Format: Paperback
Language: English
Pages: 248
Price: ₹ 175.00

(Also available in Hindi)

Author: Vishal Goyal
Format: Paperback
Language: English
Pages: 228
Price: ₹ 150.00

Author: Vishal Goyal
Format: Paperback
Language: English
Pages: 228
Price: ₹ 175.00

Chanakya was both a destructive and creative thinker able to annihilate an established empire and erect and establish another larger, richer and greater on the debris, without money, material and man. So, he is the only qualified person in human history to be Guru; Acharya; Teacher; Guide and Mentor in the field of Management. With his super mind and supreme determination he succeeded in everything and everywhere; and wrote down everything without inhibitions or secrecy for the posterity in his three monumental works:

1. Teachings of Kautilya's Arthashastra & Nitishastra
2. Perfect Analogy between Ancient Managerial System & Modern Corporate Setup

Tenali Raman was a court jester, an intelligent advisor and one of the ashtadiggajas (elephants serving as pillars and taking care of all the eight sides) in the Bhuvana Vijayam (Royal Court) of the famed Emperor of Vijayanagar Empire (City of Joy) in Karnataka – Sri Krishna Deva Raya (1509-1529), the model ruler par excellence to Ashoka, Samudra Gupta and Harsha Vardhana. Tenali Raman was an embodiment of acute wit and humour and an admirable poet of knowledge, shrewdness and ingenuity. In a short span, the legacy left behind by Tenali Raman attained eternity. All these qualities of Tenali Raman have been fully explored and displayed in this collection of vibrant fables and anecdotes.

A contemporary compilation of anecdotes Gopal Bhand for 21st Century youth in an engaging blend of wisdom and wit with social and managerial significance. The book comes packed with mind-blowing snippets to keep readers thoroughly submerged in good humour till the end of the book! It is a racy assemblage of earthly wisdom and sparking humour punctuated with moral and mind blowing perceptions to keep today's readers glued to the book looking for more and yet more!.

visit our online bookstore: **www.vspublishers.com**

Author: Bittu Kumar	Author: Anchit Barnwal	Author: V. Rajesh
Format: Paperback	Format: Paperback	Format: Paperback
Language: English	Language: English	Language: English
Pages: 136	Pages: 168	Pages: 104
Price: ₹ 120.00	Price: ₹ 200.00	Price: ₹ 120.00

"The aim of marketing is to know and understand the customer so well, the product or service fits him and sells itself."
— Peter F. Drucker

The book, Marketing for Beginners gives an exhaustive explanation about the key concepts of marketing, its strategies, and defines the important terminologies, such as Brand Selection, Distribution Channels, Vendor Selection, Pricing, Sales Process, Customer Relationship Management(CRM).

It's different and exclusive from other Marketing or Management books as it not only gives the detailed description of the various components of Marketing, but also cites examples to explain each of them, making it crystal clear to the readers.

Just as a winning podium can accommodate anyone on it, each one of us is capable to be a winner, irrespective of our shortcomings and differences. Winners' Podium – Everyone Fits on it, attempts to do just that: make out a winner amongst each one of us.

This book offers elaborate guidelines for a balanced, successful and happy living. It tells how one can find his talent, attract ideas and be successful, both personally and professionally. It also talks of happiness and the steps to it.

Through stories, anecdotes, quotations, examples and day to day observations, this book can inspire you to not only attain that most desirable success, but also to hold on and grow both internally and externally with it.

It is easy to skip a question during an exam if it is "Out of Syllabus" but what do you do if you are faced with a situation in life for which you were not given any inputs? Can you run away from the situation using the "Out of Syllabus" excuse?

Career is one area where one is expected to know and manage situations. After all a person is paid a salary to be able to handle things and deliver results. The reality is that most people get a lot of academic and conceptual inputs relating to one's career choice but very little practical inputs on how to effectively use the academic learning.

visit our online bookstore: **www.vspublishers.com**

Author: Saurabh Aggrwal
Format: Paperback
Language: English
Pages: 256
Price: ₹ 200.00

Did you know that crossword puzzles first appeared in the New York World in 1913, and soon became a popular feature in newspapers or that Kellog's as a brand had spent $90,000 on advertising, more than 100 years ago in 1906, including one $4000 a page ad in the July issue of the Ladies Home Journal, Apple had lured John Sculley away from Pepsi because they wanted him to apply his marketing skills to the personal computer market. Find facts and trivia from the world of business that will amaze and delight you. The questions in this book have been framed in a way that they are: guessable with intelligent, lateral, or lucky thinking; interesting, amusing, or surprising;

Author: S.P. Sharma
Format: Paperback
Language: English
Pages: 120
Price: ₹ 110.00

In a world marked by competition, personality is the key to success — whether it is social or business or personal or political arena. Interview for IAS or an MNC, meeting with the parents of your prospective bride, addressing a public rally, or delivering a speech in an international conference…if you have a confident and pleasing personality, you will surely make your mark! This book seeks to motivate young men and women, particularly students, to make conscious and continuous effort to build character and develop good personality.

Author: Aparna Chattopadhyay
Format: Paperback
Language: English
Pages: 184
Price: ₹ 120.00

This fascinating book authored by Dr. Aparna Chattopadhyay offers you a new vision of self-awareness which would enable you to assess your feelings, capabilities and aptitudes. As you develop self-awareness, you will not only be able to identify the emotional patterns in your life and will manage them well, but will also be able to activate all-round personality development.

This book enables you to:

- Generate fresh enthusiasm and ambition in your life
- Live more happily and effectively
- Build self-confidence and develop inner peace
- Enjoy better interpersonal relationships
- Rid yourself of unwanted negative emotions

visit our online bookstore: **www.vspublishers.com**

www.ingramcontent.com/pod-product-compliance
Lightning Source LLC
Chambersburg PA
CBHW070334230426
43663CB00011B/2307